I highly recommend *Ministry Educc* resource for faculty and leadership development in theological education. The transformative learning paradigm as clearly defined and explained in this book has significantly shaped my teaching and leadership ministries in the last ten years. No other paradigm on transformative education has been presented with a strong biblical foundation, with supporting educational research, with sensitivity to contextual realities, and with carefully designed workshops for practical application. Applying the principles of biblical transformative learning will continue to challenge the way we do education, and will continue to insist that the teacher is the curriculum!

Joanna Feliciano-Soberano, PhD
Academic Dean,
Asian Theological Seminary, Quezon City, Philippines

"Transformation" has become a meaningless catch word in ministry formation. Many use the word oblivious of its meaning. Having trained and coached leaders in transformational ministries, the authors have presented a well-researched and in-depth experience-based view of transformation – what it is, what is being transformed, by what process and with what results. The book is more of a manual for transformational training than a textbook to be studied in abstraction of practice. Consequently, those who have taken the full cycle of workshops offered by Global Associates for Transformational Education (GATE) will find this a valuable piece to guide them in their practice. For those who have not taken any or only one or two GATE workshops, I further recommend that they go through the training in order to get the best out of this material.

John Jusu, PhD
Regional Director for Africa, Overseas Council

Ministry Education That Transforms is much more than a manifesto on theological education. It is the fruit of reflection of theological educators with experience in different cultures and of their practice across cultures. It is an invitation to remember that the call of theological education is transformation, fostering the appropriation of God's truth to shape the worldview, character and practice of seminary students and of the church. This book is a must-read

BV 4020

for those who view education not as training, but as formation, and want to learn more about transformational perspectives and methods.

Elizabeth Sendek
President,
Seminario Bíblico de Colombia, Medellin, Colombia

I have known the authors of *Ministry Education That Transforms* for more than fourteen years. I can report that the lives of hundreds of faculty members in Eastern Europe, and those of their students, have been transformed through the principles and methods described in this book. The authors present methodologies and practical examples for rethinking seminary education. Here you will find a balance between high academic requirements and focus on equipping graduates for effective ministry in the church. The book stays on solid theoretical ground, yet with a practical orientation which enables theological schools in the Majority World to avoid many mistakes.

Sergiy Sannikov, PhD
Emeritus President, Euro-Asian Accrediting Association

Into the rather placid waters of a theological educator's teaching experience, this book tosses the question, "What for?" It demands that we rethink our reasons for teaching and asks that we re-purpose teaching towards transformation. Significantly, the transformation needed encompasses both tutor and taught, since to the student, "the faculty is the curriculum." Here is a book that prepares educators to prepare their students to serve the church. May its ripples increase!

Havilah Dharamraj, PhD
Academic Dean,
South Asia Institute for Advanced Christian Studies, Bengaluru, India

Traditionally, faculty development was seen only from the perspective of credentializing professors. Recognizing this as problematic has led to solving a big flaw in theological education. *Ministry Education That Transforms* represents the essence of a training project that has taken theological education to a next level, helping seminaries to be transformational and not just content providers. The GATE curriculum provides a critical answer to a real need in faculty development.

Josue Fernandez
Regional Director for Latin America and Caribbean, Overseas Council

In *Ministry Education That Transforms*, Robert Ferris, a seasoned educationist and theologian, provides a vital resource for theological educators to effect transformative teaching and learning. The reader is transitioned from theological foundations and the science and theory of learning into educational practices for designing and implementing a curriculum that transforms the learners through modeling and teaching.

To theological educators, who are mostly non-professional educators, this book provides the urgently needed educational theory and practice for transformational learning. Furthermore, this resource is a product of fifteen years of testing and refining of its philosophy and strategy for transformational education through the Global Associates for Transformational Education (GATE) workshops held in Asia, Africa, Caribbean, Eastern Europe, and Latin America.

As a GATE Associate, I highly recommend this book for use by educators and institutions who desire to see transformation of their graduates and the communities they are called to serve.

Rev Emmanuel Chemengich, DMin
Executive Director,
Association for Christian Theological Education in Africa

Many of us have heard critics say that theological education is neither theological nor educational. The reason this perception exists is the lack of teachers' training for theological educators. This book, *Ministry Education That Transforms*, is written by educators who also are theological thinkers. I highly recommend the book to those who want to see students participate in our ministry of transformation. So much of our theological education has lost its missional and ministry focus and hence we fail to see the church as a transformed and transforming community. This book is practical and has a strong theological foundation. I am convinced it will help teachers see their role as agents of transformative learning, resulting in a future more promising and a church leadership more focused on God's mission and ministry.

Ashish Chrispal, PhD
Senior Consultant, Overseas Council

ICETE Series

Ministry Education
That Transforms

ICETE International Council for Evangelical Theological Education
strengthening evangelical theological education through international cooperation

Langham
GLOBAL LIBRARY

Ministry Education That Transforms

Modeling and Teaching the Transformed Life

Robert W. Ferris

with

John R. Lillis and Ralph E. Enlow, Jr.

ICETE International Council for Evangelical Theological Education
strengthening evangelical theological education through international cooperation

Langham

GLOBAL LIBRARY

© 2018 Robert W. Ferris

Published 2018 by Langham Global Library
An imprint of Langham Publishing

Langham Partnership
PO Box 296, Carlisle, Cumbria CA3 9WZ, UK
www.langham.org

ISBNs:
978-1-78368-422-9 Print
978-1-78368-423-6 ePub
978-1-78368-424-3 Mobi
978-1-78368-425-0 PDF

British Library Cataloguing-in-Publication Data
A catalogue record for this book is available from the British Library

ISBN: 978-1-78368-422-9

Cover & Book Design: projectluz.com

Contents

Preface

The *Who, How,* and *Why* of This Book

*M*inistry Education That Transforms is the fruit of fifteen years of collaboration. Robert (Bob) Ferris, John Lillis, and Ralph Enlow are trained in biblical and theological studies and are professional educators who have invested their careers in Bible college and seminary teaching and leadership. Just as important, all have been privileged to experience extensive ministry engagement with the global church.

This combination of developed educational perspective and passion for health in the global church led them in 2003 to launch a project known as Global Associates for Transformational Education (GATE).[1] In the context of workshops with Bible college and seminary faculties, the authors interacted with hundreds of theological educators from Eastern Europe, Asia, Africa, Latin America, and the Caribbean, and honed the philosophy and strategies of transformational ministry education presented in the chapters that follow.

Although the substance of this book represents extensive group collaboration, by circumstance and mutual consent, Bob drafted most chapters. John provided a draft of chapter 3, which addresses foundational learning theory concepts and research, and an initial draft of chapter 4. Ralph's insights and editorial notes were significant in refining both the substance and the technical accuracy of the manuscript. Bob oversaw final editing.

---

1. Duane H. Elmer, Trinity Evangelical Divinity School and a member of the initial GATE team, contributed greatly to the development of GATE during its formative years. A brief account of the history of GATE can be found in appendix A.

Between 2013 and 2018, the GATE team trained new Associates, expanding from three, to six, to thirty-two. Upon completion of training for the last cohort of twenty-six new Associates from Latin America, the Caribbean, Asia, and Africa, the authors transferred leadership of GATE to their global colleagues. The educational, methodological, and cultural insights of these Associates – the rich and ever-ripening fruit of our ongoing global collaboration – are reflected throughout the book.

This book was written for our global Associates, for the faculties of seminaries that have enrolled in GATE workshops over the past fifteen years, and for those our GATE teams will train in the future. More broadly, this book is written for theological educators in the global church – both Majority World and Western – who long to see the lives of their students transformed by the power of the Word and the Spirit and who also long to see their graduates become agents of transformation in the congregations and communities where they serve. May God graciously grant that *Ministry Education That Transforms* would be used to that end.

Robert Ferris, John Lillis, and Ralph Enlow
November 2017

1

Ministry Education for a Transformed Church

Now great crowds accompanied him, and he turned and said to them, "If anyone comes to me and does not hate his own father and mother and wife and children and brothers and sisters, yes, and even his own life, he cannot be my disciple. Whoever does not bear his own cross and come after me cannot be my disciple. For which of you, desiring to build a tower, does not first sit down and count the cost, whether he has enough to complete it? . . . So therefore, any one of you who does not renounce all that he has cannot be my disciple." (Luke 14:25–28, 33)

As he was saying these things, many believed in him. So Jesus said to the Jews who had believed him, "If you abide in my word, you are truly my disciples, and you will know the truth, and the truth will set you free." (John 8:30–32)

By this my Father is glorified, that you bear much fruit and so prove to be my disciples. As the Father has loved me, so have I loved you. Abide in my love. (John 15:8–9)

Then Jesus came to them and said, "All authority in heaven and on earth has been given to me. Therefore go and make disciples of all nations, baptizing them in the name of the Father and of the

Son and of the Holy Spirit, and teaching them to obey everything
I have commanded you. And surely I am with you always, to the
very end of the age." (Matt 28:18–20 NIV)

In much of the world today, the church is growing numerically but is impotent
spiritually. Evangelical Christianity grew globally by at least 300 percent in
the four decades between 1970 and 2010.[1] Nevertheless, the superficiality of
Christianity in the global church is a troubling reality. Nations reporting the
highest percentage of Christians also are listed as the world's most corrupt.
The United States, a nation founded on explicitly Christian principles and
known for sending the highest number of cross-cultural missionaries, also is
the world's leading exporter of erotic and violent media. Western Christians,
especially in the younger generation, are abandoning the church in alarming
numbers. Across Europe, hundreds of church buildings have been converted
into mosques, taverns, and museums. Islam, not Christianity, is the world's
fastest-growing religion.[2]

Why is this? Is Christianity failing because its claims prove unsatisfying,
even unbelievable, in the crucible of twenty-first-century life? Or does the
observed failure result from widespread claims to be Christian apart from any
evidence of the transformative power of the gospel?

Missiologists recognize that Christian conversion is best identified as
worldview change.[3] In some cultures, the embedded worldview is animistic.
In much of North Africa, the Middle East, and Central Asia, the dominant
worldview is Muslim. In South and East Asia, Hindu, Buddhist, or Confucian
worldviews reign. In the West, the prevailing worldview is naturalism. Sadly,
in much of the global church, the characteristic worldview of Christians is
that of their surrounding culture. Despite their professions, the lives of the

---

1. Center for Global Christianity, "Christianity in Its Global Context: 1970–2020: Society, Religion, and Mission," Gordon-Conwell Theological Seminary, June 2013, accessed 15 March 2017, http://www.gordonconwell.edu/ockenga/research/documents/ChristianityinitsGlobalContext.pdf.

2. Michael Lipka and Conrad Hackett, "Why Muslims Are the World's Fastest Growing Religious Group," Pew Research, 6 April 2017, accessed 21 September 2017, http://www.pewresearch.org/fact-tank/2017/04/06/why-muslims-are-the-worlds-fastest-growing-religious-group/.

3. See Paul G. Hiebert, *Transforming Worldviews: An Anthropological Understanding of How People Change* (Grand Rapids: Baker Academic, 2008).

vast majority of professing Christians are hardly distinguishable from those of their non-Christian neighbors.

Why do Christian numbers grow while impact of the church on social relationships and cultural morality withers? Christians pray, national churches set and achieve church-planting goals, and theological schools graduate aspiring church leaders, yet dynamic Christianity continues to elude much of the global church.

Clearly, something must change if Christian conversion is to effect a transformed worldview and transformed lives. There are many candidates for change – a change in focus from evangelism to disciple-making, a change in church life from congregation of individuals to community of spiritual brothers and sisters, a change from witness as event to witness as lifestyle. Perhaps the most accessible change, however, is in the way candidates are prepared for church leadership.

Distressing numbers of leaders in the global church are untrained, yet many have received some formal training. In thousands of Bible schools, theological colleges, and graduate seminaries around the world, faculty members labor – often sacrificially – to transfer to students knowledge they have acquired about the Bible and about ministry in church and society. This noble effort empowers and motivates graduates to share the information, principles, and concepts they acquire with persons in the communities where they minister.

There is a critical distinction, however, between informed believers and transformed disciples. Information – especially the truth revealed in the Bible – is vitally important, but God desires truth not only to be remembered and repeated, but also to be applied in the contexts of life. God intends obedience to his truth to transform our thinking, perspectives, values, behavior, and relationships.

Faculty members desire to see the lives of their students transformed by their lectures, and pastors desire to see the lives of people in their church and community transformed by their sermons. Desire, however, does not assure realization. Indeed, singular focus on transferring information actually impedes life transformation in students and church members. To realize their desire for life transformation, faculty members and church leaders must teach and minister toward that end. This transformational commitment requires a new pedagogy and new patterns of relationships.

Transformational Ministry Education

Problems inherent in incumbent models of ministry training have been recognized for decades.[4] Some have called for abandoning traditional seminaries in favor of "church-based" ministry education.[5] Although the frustration of seminary detractors is understandable, much of the church's physical and intellectual capital, historically and currently, is invested in theological schools. Nonformal ministry training programs admirably serve some sectors within the church[6] but responsible stewardship dictates that resources represented by ministry training schools must not be discarded or dismissed. These resources must be redirected to better address the leadership needs of the church. This is a multifaceted challenge which demands understanding and ownership both by the church and by seminary faculties and administrators. Seven transitions in thinking and practice are needed to realize this goal.

From Orientation to the Guild to Orientation to the Congregation

The history of the church's romance with formal education is revealing. European universities, historically entrusted with preparing the church's ministers, often are the source and purveyors of doubt regarding the authenticity and accuracy of the Holy Scriptures and the Christian faith. In the United States, the church's tragic relationship with higher education is recounted in the history of Harvard, Yale, Princeton, University of Chicago, and many other institutions founded for the preparation of Christian ministers. Today, these institutions render little direct service to the church. Through their accrediting agencies, seminaries look largely to research universities when setting academic standards. We do well to understand the forces that contribute to this disappointing legacy.

The mission of the research university and the mission of the theological school are very different because qualifications for academic and research

---

4. F. Ross Kinsler, "Bases for Change in Theological Education," in *The Extension Movement in Theological Education*, rev. ed. (Pasadena, CA: William Carey Library, 1978, 1981), 3–24.

5. Especially vocal in advocating "church-based" ministry education as a replacement for traditional seminary education have been those associated with BILD International (http://www.bild.org/).

6. Special notice should be given to the Theological Education by Extension (TEE) movement which has been used by God in many nations. For current thinking on TEE, see https://www.increaseassociation.org/.

leadership are different from those for leadership in the church. Research universities exist to preserve and advance cultural and scientific knowledge; seminaries exist to equip leaders who, in turn, "equip the saints for the work of ministry, for building up the body of Christ" (Eph 4:12–13). When seminaries orient to the university and the scholarly guild, they equip graduates for the guild rather than for ministry in the church.

The seminary can be successful only by orienting to the church. It is the mission and leadership needs of the church, rather than the values of the university and the guild, that must dictate the seminary's culture, its curriculum, and its pedagogy. This represents a seismic shift, a tectonic realignment, in our perspective on the orientation of ministry preparation and our concept of the theological school. This change will not occur quickly or without trauma but it is essential for the health of the church and for the mission of the seminary.

From Transferring Information to Transforming Leaders

The characteristic focus of ministry education is transferring information from teachers to students. Faculty members constantly complain that they lack the time needed to "cover the material" required in their course syllabi. Although they recognize students also must develop skills, emphasis is given to acquiring and communicating information. The standard modes of student assessment are research papers and written examinations in which students are expected to rehearse or, occasionally, to synthesize what they have heard or read. Repeatedly, in workshops in Eastern Europe, Africa, Asia, and Latin America, when asked to identify the focus of the courses they teach, theological faculties indicate their primary emphasis is on transfer of knowledge and information.

This focus on information transfer is pedagogically misguided and theologically problematic. Knowledge of the Bible is critical to Christian life and ministry but acquisition, retention, and repetition of information – biblical, theological, and pastoral – is not adequate preparation for ministry. Pastors, evangelists, and missionaries do not spend their days in libraries, reading books, and writing papers; ministry is relational and Christianity is lived. Unless the truths mastered are embodied in life, they ring hollow. Unembodied truths are more apt to turn others away from Christ than to draw them to him. The marks of a Christian are not academic degrees or lists of publications but relationships of love (John 13:35) and holiness of life

(Heb 12:14). Nevertheless, life application of biblical truth – the character of the student – rarely is assessed and often is viewed as an inaccessible and inappropriate consideration in academic settings.

Focus on information transfer is also theologically problematic. The Great Commission is to "make disciples," not "teaching them *to recall* everything I have commanded you"; rather it is to teach them "*to obey* everything I have commanded you" (Matt 28:20 NIV; emphasis added). This was God's intention for Israel, as well. As Moses rehearsed God's laws and statutes for Israel, he emphasized, "you shall learn them and be careful *to do* them" (Deut 5:1; emphasis added). When we get to heaven, we will not be required to take an examination. Neither God nor Satan cares how much we know if we do not apply known truth in our lives and relationships.

In addition, singular focus on information transfer is misdirected. New Testament qualification for church leadership is most specifically addressed in 1 Timothy 3:1–13; 2 Timothy 2:24–25; and Titus 1:6–9. Analysis of the qualities listed in these passages reveals that mastery of information is mentioned only once ("[The elder] must hold firm to the trustworthy word as taught," Titus 1:9), a few skills are mentioned (e.g. "able to teach," "manage his own household well"), but an abundance of qualifications listed relate to the character of the leader (e.g. "sober-minded, self-controlled, respectable, hospitable . . . gentle, not quarrelsome"). Character is shaped life-on-life, not simply by teaching standards or imposing rules. Information – especially biblical revelation – has instrumental value; it acquires value and importance as it is applied in life.

To align pedagogy with theology does not require that information be devalued but rather that it be applied. The goal of ministry training should be obedience to truth, not simply recall of truth. Obedience to truth opens the life of a believer – and, most critically, a seminary student – to the transformative power of the Holy Spirit. When faculty members teach for obedience to truth, they create environments in which ministry education can be transformative.

From School to Learning Community

European, North American, and colonial patterns of education have been profoundly shaped by Hellenistic perspectives and philosophy. Central in that respect is individualism, the assumption that the good of the individual takes precedence over the good of the community and that the community will prosper as individuals within the community prosper. This assumption undergirds Western valuing of democracy and capitalism. Nowhere is individualism more evident, however, than in the school. As in Plato's *Republic*, students are sorted and promoted based on their individual abilities and achievements. Elite status is assigned to teachers and "those who know." Progress in schooling is viewed as a self-justifying good and those who progress farthest in school are esteemed in society and in the academy.

The ancient Hebrews viewed life differently. Like in Majority World cultures today, priority was assigned to pursuing the good of the community. As the community prospered, it was assumed, individuals within the community also would prosper. Highest value was assigned to *shalom*, to life as God intends. The word *shalom* is much richer than our English word "peace" which often translates it. *Shalom* includes physical health and safety, provision of personal, family, and community needs, congenial relationships within family and community, and general well-being. In the community characterized by *shalom*, each is his brother's keeper. Commerce is conducted with fair weights and measures and a member of the community is not charged interest. The vulnerable of society, the widow and the orphan, are protected and their needs provided for by the community. Love privileges the good of the other above one's own.

Schooling inherently promotes individual values rather than fostering a nurturing community. Intentional steps must be taken to redress the school's bias toward unbiblical individualism. While recognizing differences in learners' giftings and roles, teachers should model and encourage valuing each individual, caring for one another, and commitment to community. Too often, our churches simply are congregations of individuals. The seminary campus may afford the best opportunity for students to experience community and *shalom*. That will not happen, however, unless – collectively – we take steps to minimize expressions of our academic bias toward individualism, to promote a community mindset, and to care for one another as God intends.

From Competitive Environment to Collaborative Culture

One of the more troublesome effects of individualism in traditional schooling is its promotion of learning as a competitive endeavor. It is the teacher's privilege and responsibility to "grade" students and their work. Since only one student can be best in any class, egocentric competition provides motivation to excel, yielding a limited number of winners, and many losers left with doubts about themselves and their abilities. Collaboration or assistance rendered to another typically is viewed as "cheating" and is punished accordingly. Advancement above one's peers and praise from "those who know" are goals to be attained.

Again, the biblical model is different; collaboration, rather than competition, is prized. In Israel, education was collaborative as the people of Israel taught God's law to their households and their neighbors.

If our education is to be Christian, teachers must find ways to nurture collaborative attitudes and activities. We must be more aware of our fallen tendencies toward egocentric self-promotion at the expense of others and to train our students to avoid these sinful attitudes and behaviors. Rather than focusing primarily on individual achievements, we should prioritize celebrating the health of the class, the community, and the church – as well as those who contribute to it. This demands deep reflection, however, on the culture of our schools and seminaries.

From Faculty as Elite Scholars to Faculty as Wise Models

The university has been an unfaithful handmaiden of the church. The culture of the university is the domain of the scholarly guild. Knowledge is prized above all else – preservation of knowledge, transmission of knowledge, and discovery and extension of knowledge. All this is appropriate; Western society benefits from the substantial contributions of the university. Yet when the values of the university and the guild are adopted by seminaries, the effect on the seminary's mission is disastrous.

The values of the guild are sharply at odds with the values of the church and the primary qualifications for spiritual leadership. Seminary education need not despise knowledge or privilege ignorance but it does need to recognize that knowledge has instrumental (versus intrinsic) value. God's truth becomes transformative as it is applied in life and society. The ideal seminary faculty member, therefore, is not the detached scholar but the engaged minister.

To recover its mission, the seminary must reassess the qualifications and expectations of its faculty. The controlling principle was stated twenty centuries ago: "every one when he is fully taught will be like his teacher" (Luke 6:40 RSV). Biblical standards for entrance to ministry principally are issues of character, rather than advanced knowledge. Knowledge of God and his revelation are essential but Hebraic knowledge, as we have seen, transcends mere recall; it demands obedience to truth known. The primary qualification for seminary teachers, therefore, must be their obedience to and modeling of the truths they teach. Similarly, the focus of their instruction must be to see the truth of Scripture lived out in the lives of their students. Recall of biblical truth is important for both faculty members and students, but it is not sufficient. To be transformative, truth must be demonstrated in individual and community relationships of love, moral purity, and justice.

From Educational Achievement to Ministry Effectiveness

Because schooling and schoolers focus on academic achievement and awards, these are the standards applied when assessing learners. Initially, this is seen in assessing applicants to the school or seminary. While inquiry may be made about the applicant's relationship to Christ and to a local church, primary consideration typically is assigned to the applicant's prior experience and success in schooling. Similarly, both course grades and the awarding of certificates or degrees focus on a student's academic achievement.

Why is this not viewed as problematic when the biblical standards for church leadership are not academic but issues of character, spiritual giftedness, and evidence of faithfulness in ministry? If the seminary affirms its calling to prepare ministers for the church, it seems clear that academic success must be revalued. The spiritual and moral equipping of church leaders in training must be assigned new priority. This reprioritization will be evidenced first in revised standards of admission. In a learning environment where obedience to biblical truth is taught and modeled, a student who already evidences gifts and qualities for church leadership prior to entry is more likely to progress in developing those qualities than is a student without this advantage.

This standard also must be applied upon completion of the seminary program. Students who achieve high marks in scholarship but who resist God's work in their lives or who evidence little aptitude or gifting for ministry should not be certified for church leadership. Only as schools own their mission to develop leaders for the church, and as faculty members own their responsibility to teach for life and ministry transformation, can such a standard be imposed. When instruction is transformational, however, it is reasonable and fair to assess learners on evidence of transformed attitudes and behaviors observed in their lives.

From Assessing Inputs, Processes, and Outputs to Assessing Social Impact

In addition to assessment of students, criteria and methods of assessing the seminary's curricula and program of training also must be reconsidered. Historically, educational institutions, including seminaries, have reported information about resources for teaching and learning ("input data"). Statistics and reports are provided on incoming students' academic qualifications, faculty academic qualifications, learning resources (including, but not limited to, library holdings), physical facilities dedicated to instruction, faculty/student ratios, and curriculum proportions and design. More rigorous assessment also has examined the methods of instruction employed, graduation rates, and the placement of graduates in ministry (often termed "process and output" data). Focus on input, process, and output assessment, however, can lead to inappropriate conclusions about the appropriateness and effectiveness of the training offered.

The ultimate criterion for assessing the training provided by a seminary is the way individual believers, local churches, and communities are changed as a result of their graduates' ministries. If a seminary boasts high graduation and placement rates but the churches and communities where graduates serve are unchanged by the gospel, how can we be satisfied that the seminary is fulfilling its mission?

God intends that the effect of the redemption which he has purchased and which we proclaim should result in lives of humility and holiness, and in communities marked by justice, compassion, and righteousness. When we see this as the effect of the ministry of a seminary's graduates, it is fair to conclude that the training offered is transformational and the school's programs are aligned with its mission.

Rethinking Seminary Education

This chapter began with the observation that the global church falls far short of impacting local and global cultures as God intends and that rethinking seminary education may afford the most accessible approach to redressing this inadequacy. Although we have observed seven specific areas in which change is needed to realize transformational ministry training, these changes are within our grasp. It is not necessary to abandon the seminary to realize our goal of a vital and transformative church.[7] Nevertheless, profound adjustments in our approach to seminary education are needed, and these changes will not come easily. May God embolden and enable us to trust him for the challenges at hand.

---

7. Global Associates for Transformational Education (GATE) is a project that enables faculties to make the shift from teaching only for information transfer to teaching for life and ministry transformation. The history of GATE is related in appendix A and the educational values that have guided development of GATE are described in appendix B. GATE teams work with clusters of schools, providing a curriculum facilitated in four three-day workshops offered at one-year intervals. GATE's curriculum is briefly described in appendix C and a typical Year 1 workshop schedule is provided in appendix D. For more about GATE, see www.GATEglobal.org.

2

Teaching for Transformation: Theological Foundations

When rethinking seminary education for transformational leadership in church and community, there is no better place to begin than with the Scriptures. Educational wisdom constantly adapts and develops in response to research findings and emerging theory but God's Word provides an unchanging criterion for assessing educational values, theories, and methods. What we find, when we examine the Scriptures – both the Old and New Testaments – is that God intends his truth to transform our lives, our relationships, and, thereby, our societies.

Education in Ancient Israel was Transformative by Design

As Moses rehearsed God's faithfulness and God's law prior to Israel's entry into the promised land, his repeated emphasis was on the critical importance of adherence to God's law. It was not enough to have received God's law or to remember God's law; Israel was *to do* God's law (i.e. to allow obedience to God's law to transform every aspect of their individual and community lives).[1] This transformative learning was to occur, furthermore, in the family and in the community.

---

1. The expression "be careful to do [God's law]" occurs twenty times in Deuteronomy.

The Purpose of Education Was to Know and Obey God's Law

Barclay cites the Mishnah as teaching that "the threefold duty of a father is 'to instruct his son in the Law, to bring him into wedlock, and to teach him a handicraft.'"[2] The ancient Jews recognized that a man's moral education was as essential as preparation for marriage or a means of livelihood. The text for one's moral enlightenment was God's law, given through Moses. Intimate familiarity with and obedience to the law was essential for acceptance by God and his blessing. A father's love for his son was reflected in teaching him to know and obey God's law.

Because obedience to the law was the focus of education among the Hebrews, the primary qualifications for teaching the law entailed both an accurate familiarity with the law and a lifestyle of obedience to the law. Because the law was designed to be transformative, molding the character of the learner to alignment with the character of God, it was essential that a father – the teacher – should model the obedience desired. Barclay notes, "The Jews were much more concerned about the moral character of the teacher than they were about his academic qualifications."[3]

For the Hebrews, the purpose of learning was transformation, realized as truth incorporated into life. This contrasted sharply with the Hellenistic ideal of learning for the sake of acquiring knowledge. The Greeks assumed that knowledge acquired would lead naturally to life change, even though each of us recognizes we know better than we do. The Hebrews, in contrast, understood that truth must be enacted in the life of the learner before it is acknowledged as learned. Thus, whereas the Hellenistic perspective focused on acquisition of knowledge, the Hebraic perspective sought transformation observed. In the biblical perspective, true learning is transformative.

The Context of Education Was Family and Community Life

In ancient Israel, primary responsibility for education of children rested with their parents. The synagogue school was unknown in Israel prior to the exile, so education occurred in the context of the home and daily life. Moses commands parents to meditate on God's commandments and to "teach them diligently to

---

2. William Barclay, *Educational Ideals in the Ancient World* (Grand Rapids: Baker, 1959), 16.
3. Barkley, *Educational Ideals*, 44.

your children, [to] talk of them when you sit in your house, and when you walk by the way, and when you lie down, and when you rise" (Deut 6:6–7; cf. 11:19). Later he envisions a context in which children inquire about the meaning of their way of life and parents rehearse the history of God's deliverance of his people and the giving of the law (Deut 6:20–25). Because education occurred in the context of the family and of daily life, acquisition of knowledge as an academic pursuit was unknown. Learning was directed toward obedience to the law and transformation of character.

Although this was the intent, the ancient Hebrews were not exempt from human fallenness. The law was not always obeyed and not all lives were transformed. Indeed, God chides Israel for their stubbornness and calls them to fear him, to walk in all his ways, to love him, to serve him with all their heart, and to keep his commandments (Deut 10:12–16). The foolish son, the son who despised the law rather than allowing it to transform his life, brought grief to his parents (Prov 10:1; 17:25). Similarly, God expressed grief over the refusal of his people to obey him (Ezek 18:30–32).

The family was the primary context for education in ancient Israel but it was not the only context in which teaching and learning was pursued. In contrast to his contemporary context of mutual instruction, Jeremiah envisions a future kingdom in which "no longer shall each one teach his neighbor and each his brother, saying, 'Know the Lord,' for they shall all know me . . ." (Jer 31:34). Moral instruction was a common pursuit that occurred in community.

The Hebrew priest's primary responsibility was to attend to the temple ritual and to offer sacrifices but he also had educational responsibility. After Nadab and Abihu, the sons of Aaron, were judged by God for profaning the sacrifice, God told Aaron, "You are to distinguish between the holy and the common, and between the unclean and the clean, and you are to teach the people of Israel all the statutes that the Lord has spoken to them by Moses" (Lev 10:10–11). Throughout the Old Testament, we find other references that indicate priests exercised a teaching role (see 2 Kgs 17:27–28; 2 Chr 15:3; Ezra 7:10; Ezek 44:23; Mic 3:11). God desires righteousness and justice, health and prosperity (i.e. *shalom*) for his people, and the means is knowledge of his law, situated in community, taught by God himself, but also by parents, neighbors, and priests. As God's law is integrated into life, life is transformed.

Jesus Modeled Transformative Teaching

The transformed life was God's intent but Israel was a stubborn people. (Aren't we all!) Transformation into the character of God demands surrendering our self-centeredness and self-control. Through the exile, Israel finally learned the folly of pursuing other gods but they remained unready to submit to God's purpose and desire. Rather than allowing God's law to transform them into his image, they domesticated the law, reducing it to a catalog of actions to be observed or avoided. Then they built "hedges" about the law, interpretations and further regulations – an oral law – to guard against violation of the revealed and written law. About AD 200, Rabbi Judah the Prince codified this oral law in 248 positive and 365 negative commandments, known as the Mishnah. By observing these 613 commands, one could be satisfied that one had "kept" the law while remaining untouched by its transformative power.

Jesus's Goal Was Transformation of Life for Relationship with God

Jesus condemned this abuse of God's law which focused on recall and legalistic observance rather than life transformation. When asked by Pharisees – the strictest sect of his day – why his disciples did not observe the oral law, Jesus pointed out their hypocrisy. He observed, "You leave the commandment of God and hold to the tradition of men," and continued, "You have a fine way of rejecting the commandment of God in order to establish your tradition!" (Mark 7:6–9). Rejecting the law? Their intent was not to reject the law but to assure they had kept it! Nevertheless, by domesticating the law, by reducing it to something they could superficially perform, they stripped it of its transformative power.

On another occasion, after legal experts quizzed Jesus on points of the law, Jesus named their hypocrisy (Matt 22:15–40). Because of their legalism, he pronounced their proselytes "twice as much a child of hell" as the Pharisees themselves (Matt 23:13–15). They were blind fools whose interpretations of the law failed to discern that God alone is holy and it was his presence that made holy the temple, the sacrifice, and all that was associated with it (Matt 23:16–22). In their obsession with technical precision, they focused on minutiae and ignored the profound and the life-changing (Matt 23:23–24). They attended to externals, that which is apparent to others, and tolerated hidden lawlessness

(Matt 23:25–26). They were keen for religious observance but were damned by their legalistic distortion of the law, nullifying its transformative intent (Matt 23:29–36).

It was not God's law to which Jesus objected; indeed, he affirmed the slightest detail of the law and claimed that he came to bring the law to its fulfillment (Matt 5:17–18). He commended strict adherence to God's law but noted that its intent reached beyond legalistic observance to life transformation (Matt 5:19–20). With six specific examples (Matt 5:21–48) Jesus highlighted the transformative intent of God's law.

Other religious leaders in Israel had disciples, but Jesus's call to discipleship was different. He called his disciples to be with him (Mark 3:14). They observed his private life and his public ministry (Mark 3:20 – 6:6) and then he sent them to do as he had done (Mark 6:7–13). Rather than domesticating the law, Jesus pointed out the cost of transformative obedience (Luke 9:57–62). He also modeled embrace of that cost, accepting rejection and crucifixion.

Jesus's Teaching Methods Were Transformative

Throughout his years of ministry, Jesus was recognized as a teacher. It is the most common way he was addressed. Yet Jesus's approach to teaching was different from that of other religious teachers, to the amazement of all who heard him (Mark 1:22). His teaching, when received and obeyed, had transformative power (see Luke 19:1–10).

Jesus employed methods of teaching that were transformative. He engaged his listeners by teaching in the context of daily life and by employing situations with which his contemporaries were familiar. "A sower went out to sow . . ." (Matt 13:3): living in an agrarian society, every first-century Jew had observed that situation repeatedly. "Two men went up into the temple to pray . . ." (Luke 18:10): Jesus was on the way to Jerusalem as he introduced that story. Those traveling with him had, themselves, entered the temple to pray. They immediately could identify with the scene Jesus painted.

Jesus also used spontaneous events as occasions to teach spiritual lessons. "Now he was teaching in one of the synagogues on the Sabbath. And behold, there was a woman who had had a disabling spirit for eighteen years" (Luke 13:10–11). Jesus seized the opportunity to teach the relative importance of legal adherence and mercy for those who suffer (cf. Mark 3:1–6). A stormy lake provided the context for a lesson on faith (Mark 4:35–41). Jesus capitalized on the inability of his disciples to free an epileptic boy from demonic oppression to teach the power of prayer (Mark 9:14–20). The disciples' debate over which of them was greatest provided the occasion for a lesson on humility (Mark 9:33–37). A rich man's option to abandon discipleship provided the context for a lesson on the deceptiveness of wealth (Mark 10:17–27). A question about taxes, designed to entrap him, afforded an opportunity to teach discernment regarding obligations (Mark 12:13–17). In all of these situations (and many more), Jesus's listeners were immediately engaged because they were part of the context. Jesus's teaching was not separated from life.

Jesus also engaged his listeners by his use of story. Parables, Jesus's most common mode of teaching, were stories with embedded spiritual lessons. Recognizing the spiritual truth hidden in Jesus's parables required effort on the part of his hearers. Many did not invest the needed effort. For them, Jesus's parables simply were stories without meaning. Others, however, recognized the truths taught and benefited spiritually (see Matt 13:10–17, 34–35). A foundational educational principle recognizes that transformative learning occurs only when learners are engaged. Jesus's frequent use of story – and, particularly, stories with hidden meaning – was an effective way of engaging his listeners and teaching the truths they needed to hear.

Jesus was a master at asking probing questions. Zuck lists 225 unduplicated questions recorded in the four Gospels that were asked by Jesus.[4] Many of Jesus's questions were open questions; the answer depended upon the one asked. "If you love those who love you, what reward do you have?" (Matt 5:46; Luke 6:32). "Why did you doubt?" (Matt 14:31). "What do you want me to do for you?" (Matt 20:32; Mark 10:51; Luke 18:41). "What are you discussing together as you walk along?" (Luke 24:17 NIV). Jesus's questions evoked thought, they exposed unchallenged assumptions, they pointed to unarticulated truths. As Horne observes, "[Jesus] came not to answer questions but to ask them; not to settle men's souls but to provoke them; not to save men from problems but to save them from indolence; not to make life easier but to make it more educative."[5] We could add: not to fill their minds but to transform their lives.

---

4. Roy B. Zuck, *Teaching as Jesus Taught* (Grand Rapids: Baker, 1995), 258–276.
5. Herman Horne, *Jesus the Teacher* (Grand Rapids: Kregel, 1998), 55.

Jesus's teaching also is seeded with provocative statements that invite reflection. "You strain out a gnat but swallow a camel," he told the Pharisees (Matt 23:24 NIV). On another occasion he said, "Many who are first will be last, and the last first" (Matt 19:30), and in so doing indicated that the ethic of the kingdom inverts the values of the current age. He told his disciples, "Whoever would be great among you must be your servant, and whoever would be first among you must be your slave" (Matt 20:26–27). What does that mean! And he warns, "Whoever exalts himself will be humbled, and whoever humbles himself will be exalted" (Matt 23:12). Hmm.

Jesus also included many aphorisms in his teaching, bits of wisdom that have broad application and so serve to remind listeners of the point of his teaching. "Tomorrow will worry about itself. Each day has enough trouble of its own" (Matt 6:34 NIV). Who can forget "Where your treasure is, there your heart will be also" (Matt 6:21)? Jesus dramatically tied speech to one's moral condition when he noted, "The mouth speaks what the heart is full of" (Matt 12:34 NIV). Ouch! And "All who draw the sword will die by the sword" (Matt 26:52 NIV). Jesus employed such memorable statements because he wanted his hearers to reflect on the meaning for their lives. Jesus clearly intended to impact the lives of his hearers.

Jesus Modeled the Transformed Life

In chapter 5, we will explore the critical importance of the teacher as model; Jesus understood this principle and employed it effectively.

Jesus taught his followers to trust God but he also modeled a life of faith. When a storm was blowing and his disciples feared drowning at sea, Jesus chided them for their lack of faith and – by faith! – stilled the storm (Matt 8:23–26). When the disciples were amazed that a tree had withered overnight, Jesus responded, "If you have faith and do not doubt, you will not only do what has been done to the fig tree, but even if you say to this mountain, 'Be taken up and thrown into the sea,' it will happen" (Matt 21:21). Jesus never said, "The reason you cannot do the things I do is because you are not God, as I am." Rather, he said, "Truly, truly, I say to you, whoever believes in me will also do the works that I do; and greater works than these will he do, because I am going to the Father" (John 14:12).

Jesus also modeled a life of prayer. Repeatedly, throughout his ministry, he retreated for times of prayer (Mark 1:35; Matt 14:23; Luke 5:15–16). Before choosing the twelve disciples, he spent the night in prayer (Luke 6:12–16). Jesus's transfiguration occurred on what began as a prayer retreat with his three closest friends (Luke 9:28–29). When the disciples asked Jesus why they were unable to heal an epileptic child, Jesus told them that prayer was the only effective recourse (Mark 9:28–29). As he anticipated his death by crucifixion, Jesus chose to spend his final hours in prayer (Matt 26:36–39). Because they observed Jesus's life of prayer, the disciples asked him to teach them to pray (Luke 11:1).

Jesus modeled humility and servanthood. He chided his disciples for their preoccupation with greatness and warned them that pursuit of prominence is inconsistent with the ethic of his kingdom (Matt 20:25–27). He drove his message home, however, by pointing to his own example of servanthood (Matt 20:28). On the night prior to his death, Jesus modeled humility and servanthood by washing the feet of the disciples (John 13:2–11). Lest they miss the significance of his example, however, he charged them to do as he had done (John 13:12–17).

Throughout his ministry, Jesus modeled compassion and selfless love. When Jesus saw the crowds, "he had compassion for them, because they were harassed and helpless, like sheep without a shepherd" (Matt 9:36). Compassion moved Jesus to heal the sick (Matt 14:14), to provide food for the faint (Matt 15:32), to open the eyes of the blind (Matt 20:34),[6] to heal a leper (Mark 1:41–42), and to raise the dead (Luke 7:13–15). Jesus was deeply moved by the grief of Martha and Mary and he wept at the tomb of Lazarus (John 11:33–35). Later he wept as he considered God's judgment on Jerusalem, the center of Israel's religious establishment (Matt 23:37–39). Jesus's compassion arose from his love for people. We are specifically told that Jesus loved the rich young ruler (Mark 10:21), that he loved Martha, Mary, and Lazarus (John 11:5), that John was "the disciple whom [Jesus] loved" (John 19:26), and that he unconditionally

---

6. The word translated "pity" in the ESV is the one elsewhere translated "compassion." Also in Mark 1:41.

and unreservedly loved[7] "his own," those who identified with him (John 13:1). As John reflected on Jesus's life and death he came to understand the essence of divine love. Phillips's translation captures John's profound recognition of the extent of Jesus's love: "We know and, to some extent realise, the love of God for us because Christ expressed it in laying down his life for us" (1 John 3:16). Indeed, Jesus said that the love he modeled would be the distinguishing characteristic of his disciples (John 13:34–35).

Jesus faced life as we do, yet he modeled a life of holiness (Heb 4:15). When attacked by the Pharisees, the guardians of righteousness in his day, Jesus challenged them to convict him of sin and they could not (John 8:46). The disciples who lived with him for three years and who were closest to him testified to his sinlessness. Peter wrote, "He committed no sin, neither was deceit found in his mouth" (1 Pet 2:22). John also testified, "in him there is no sin" (1 John 3:5). Paul, inspired by the Holy Spirit, wrote, "For our sake he made him to be sin who knew no sin, so that in him we might become the righteousness of God" (2 Cor 5:21). Because Jesus lived a holy life, he could remind us that God's standard is perfection (Matt 5:48). Peter also notes that God's standard for us is his own holiness (1 Pet 1:16) and he points us to Jesus, "a lamb without blemish or spot" (1 Pet 1:19) as our redeemer.

Finally, Jesus modeled kingdom priority and intentional obedience. So often, life in the twenty-first century seems chaotic and scattered. Distractions abound. Jesus was not distracted. From the beginning of his ministry to the very end, he proclaimed that the kingdom of God was at hand (Mark 1:14–15; 14:25). He recognized proclamation of God's kingship as the purpose of his life and ministry (Luke 4:43) and urged those who would follow his example to pursue God's kingdom as their highest priority (Luke 9:59–62). Jesus knew and pursued his mission, undeterred by threats or dangers (Luke 13:31–33). As his earthly ministry neared its end, "his face was set toward Jerusalem" (Luke 9:53): he would not be deterred from his mission of redemption. His demonstration of intentional obedience and kingdom priority was so compelling that his disciples would choose, if necessary, to die with him (John 11:16).

---

7. This is the most probable meaning of the expression translated by the ESV as "he loved them to the end."

As we examine the method of Jesus the teacher, we see that modeling lay at the heart of Jesus's ministry. He was God incarnate, the perfect revelation of the Father because he and the Father were one (John 1:14). To have seen him was to have seen the Father (John 14:9). As he taught truth about God and our human condition, he also modeled the truths he taught. He showed us what it means to live a life of faith, prayer, humility, and servanthood. He demonstrated the meaning of selfless love, not only in his death on the cross but in his many acts of compassion toward the suffering, the oppressed, and the lost. He also proved that a life of holiness is possible and that intentional obedience to God and prioritization of his kingdom is the path of submission and sonship.

Throughout the Scriptures and specifically in the life and ministry of Jesus we see that God's intention is that we should be transformed by truth. Truth, integrated into life, has transformative power. Life transformation was God's intention in giving the law to Moses and it was the method and message of Jesus.

Although seminary education too often has reflected a Hellenistic pursuit of information and a Pharisaic obsession with detail, we can and must redirect ministry education toward obedience to truth taught and modeled. Thankfully, the best educators also have recognized principles that point in the same direction.

3

Teaching for Transformation: The Science of Learning

Transformational ministry education is grounded in an understanding of principles that underlie the teaching–learning process. During the last hundred years, understanding of that process has greatly expanded through the work of researchers and theorists as they have focused on various aspects of the science of learning. This research and the resulting development of learning theory has provided insight teachers can use to facilitate learning. A basic understanding of both the science of learning and the methods of teaching enables educators to design more effective, transformative learning experiences. This chapter offers a brief survey of the research and theories that inform ministry education that transforms.

Piaget: Disequilibrium as the Gateway to Learning

Jean Piaget, a Swiss psychologist, is most noted for his research on the cognitive development of children. Piaget concluded that human learners are active agents, creating an understanding of the world around them, rather than passive responders shaped by external stimuli as assumed by behavioral psychologists.[1] He asserted that from birth children construct mental models of their world. The basic building blocks of these models (Piaget labeled them *psychic schema*)

---

1. Leading behavioral psychologists include Ivan Pavlov, Edward Thorndike, and B. F. Skinner.

take into account objects (persisting and moving) and recurring events – that is, patterns dealing with space, time, material, and motion. These mental models provide the framework for any contemplated course of action; they are the bases for fore-seeing, fore-thinking, and fore-planning.

Piaget observed that as children develop they become agents in their own cognitive development. They obtain and organize learning experiences in order to expand their mental model and gain a fuller understanding of the world in which they live.[2] These experiences "key" the formation of their *schema*. The most fundamental and persistent process of learning and growth is *assimilation*. Assimilation entails absorbing, organizing, and integrating into the existing schema new experiences and information around the activities which produce them. Many situations or objects resist the activity patterns a child tries on them. In response, the child may attempt an alternative activity. You may recall, as a child, trying to fit pieces of a simple puzzle into pre-cut spaces. The child may attempt to fit a square puzzle piece into a circular space – and keep trying until realizing the object and the space don't match. The mental process of modifying the existing schema to take into account input that does not fit an existing mental model is called *accommodation*. As accommodation modifies the existing schema and creates a new schema, children are able to assimilate new data and gain a more expansive understanding of the world in which they live. Cognitive growth and development occur as the dual processes of *assimilation* and *accommodation* lead into ever-more successful *adaptation* to a child's external world.

Piaget noted that cognitive growth and development does not occur at a steady rate over time but irregularly with significant stops and starts. He described a state of *equilibrium* as one in which an individual's existing schema processes most new information through *assimilation*. When new experiences or information cannot reasonably be made to fit an existing schema, however, a discomforting state of *disequilibrium* occurs. Because humans – children, adolescents, and adults – are intolerant of the mental frustration caused by *disequilibrium*, they seek a new state of *equilibrium* by modifying the existing

---

2. For example, infants may follow with their eyes, turn their head, explore with hands and mouth, grip, pull, push, or explore jointly and alternately with eye and hand. A child will repeat an activity that leads to an interesting experience and either go on from there or return to it again.

schema to account for the new information (i.e. by *accommodation*). The new schema will persist until experience again effects disequilibrium.

Disequilibration – creating disequilibrium as a context for learning – can be a powerful teaching–learning tool. Mental tension or cognitive disorientation occurs when there is a discrepancy or lack of fit between what people believe and what is presented to them. Jesus often created or took advantage of this tension to help his disciples see him as he truly was, to see the kingdom as it truly is, and to see life situations through "kingdom eyes." The Sermon on the Mount (Matt 5–7) illustrates how Jesus created disequilibrium by contradicting well-accepted teachings of the time. Using the phrases "you have heard that it was said" and "but I tell you," Jesus challenged his listeners to reconsider and modify their current understanding of God's truth. Listeners were unable to *assimilate* his teachings into their current understandings of God's law. Upon hearing "unless your righteousness exceeds that of the scribes and Pharisees, you will never enter the kingdom of heaven" (Matt 5:20), those following Jesus experienced disequilibration and were forced to rethink (i.e. to *accommodate*) their concept of righteousness.[3]

Freire and Vella: Dialogue Education and Empowerment

Dialogue education entails continuous conversation and communication between the teacher and the learners. It involves more than an occasional discussion question thrown in to engage the learners during a teaching presentation. The teacher uses ongoing dialogue to gain insight into learners' current perspectives, ideas, and possible misunderstandings on a topic. Learners also have an opportunity to investigate and enhance their understanding while learning to use language to build on existing knowledge. Although teaching through dialogue can be traced to Socrates, interest in the approach was revived in the 1970s. Two educators who have contributed significantly to dialogue education theory and practice are Paulo Freire and Jane Vella.

---

3. For other examples of Jesus's use of disequilibration, see the Kingdom Parables (Matt 13), the Bread of Life Discourse (John 6), the Olivet Discourse (Matt 24–25), and the Upper Room Discourse (John 13–17).

Paulo Freire

Freire was a Brazilian educator who has significantly influenced educational thought and practice. Freire[4] believed that all persons, no matter how "ignorant" or uneducated, through dialogue with others could learn to interpret, understand, engage, and then transform their world. His concept of education was built on belief in the centrality and necessity of dialogue for educational transformation. He developed this approach (a "pedagogy of the oppressed") in order to "liberate" those who were poor, often illiterate, and unable to change their circumstances (the "oppressed"). The goal of the dialogic process was that learners might "discover" themselves as persons; that is, that they might acquire an existential awareness of their ability to impact their context significantly and to understand their role in that process. Freire labeled development of this world and self-awareness *conscientization.*

Freire did not believe conscientization could be accomplished through incumbent models of formal education because, in his opinion, authentic dialogue must be egalitarian. Teachers and learners must view themselves as equals, working together in a spirit of mutual respect. Teachers cannot dialogue from a position of perceived superiority or power. In traditional approaches to education, Freire argued, the educational institution is a depository of knowledge learners must acquire. Teachers, as proprietors of that knowledge, "deposit" information into the learners and are entitled to "withdraw" this knowledge on demand. This "banking" approach to education does not lead learners to critical reflection necessary for true growth, awareness of their personhood, or capacity to change their world.

For Freire, learning does not end simply with an enhanced understanding and self-awareness. Knowledge acquired and values developed should lead to informed action, or "praxis," that has potential to transform learners' circumstances. Because he believed that traditional, formal education could not and would not lead to conscientization, Freire designed a nonformal education approach to teaching. He emphasized that dialogue is essential for facilitators to understand the context of learners and that only egalitarian dialogue can empower learners to discover their capacity to understand and change their world.

---

4. See Paulo Freire, *Pedagogy of the Oppressed* (New York: Seabury, 1970).

Jane Vella

Vella went to Tanzania in 1956 as a Catholic Maryknoll Sister and spent the next twenty-five years facilitating adult literacy and community education in Tanzania and internationally. Vella met Freire and was greatly influenced by his concept of education as dialogue. During her years in Tanzania, Vella "operationalized" Freire's theory, developing a practical approach she labeled "dialogue education." Whereas Freire's style is often opaque, Vella offers clearly explained principles and methods for applying Freire's insights.[5] This is Vella's major contribution to adult education. Two specific areas in which she provides practical guidance are her emphases on "learning tasks" and "the eight steps of planning."

Vella argues that education should focus on "learning tasks" (what learners do) rather than on "teaching tasks" (what teachers do) or on "learning goals" (what teachers expect that learners will be able to do). In "teaching tasks," only the teacher is an active participant, presenting what is to be learned. The passive learners' task is to listen and to retain what is presented. "Learning goals" turn out to be just a more thoughtful form of "teaching tasks," since student learning is not demonstrated. A "learning task," in contrast, is "an open question put to learners who have all the resources they need to respond."[6] To the extent that learning tasks are egalitarian, the knowledge of both learners and teachers is relevant to the task. Students bring knowledge of past experience and knowledge of their present context. The teacher brings knowledge of past experience as well but also brings knowledge of the subject matter, its philosophical context and practical implications. Whether the intent is to provide new information or to stimulate learners to relate knowledge to life situations, a learning task should insure that learners are actively engaged and are able to access and utilize all the resources needed for learning.

---

5. See Jane Vella, *Learning to Listen, Learning to Teach*, rev. ed. (San Francisco: Jossey-Bass, 2002), in which Vella identifies and illustrates twelve principles that underlie "dialogue education." For Vella's most comprehensive statement of her thinking, see *On Teaching and Learning* (San Francisco: Jossey-Bass, 2008).

6. Jane Vella, *Taking Learning to Task* (San Francisco: Jossey-Bass, 2001), 9.

A second area where Vella offers practical guidance is her "eight steps of planning."[7] The steps are framed as eight questions:

1. Who? – participants, leaders, the number of participants
2. Why? – the participants' motives for learning
3. When? – the time frame; when and how long
4. Where? – the physical site, including resources available
5. So that? – the anticipated change
6. What? – the content: skills, knowledge, attitudes
7. What for? – achievement-based objectives
8. How? – learning tasks and resources

The order of these steps is significant; in dialogue education, the first four questions must be addressed before determining the content to be taught. This reverses common practice in most formal education. When assigned to teach a course, most teachers spring immediately to the "What?" (i.e. What will I teach? What is the content I will cover?). Vella's "eight steps of planning" alert teachers that there are prior questions to be addressed and that failure to consider those may lead to inappropriate decisions regarding content.

The fifth step, "So that?," acknowledges that teachers bring their own values and intentions, often constrained by mandated curricular goals and institutional values, to the teaching–learning event. The teacher's goals are shaped by information about the learners (Steps 1–4) when determining the content of the course or lesson. Historically, teachers were advised to begin by clarifying their teaching objectives. Vella alerts us that information regarding our learners should inform our instructional goals. Together, information about the learners and candid recognition of our instructional goals guide selection of the content to be taught – the "What?"

Vella's seventh step, "What for?," asserts that learning objectives must be "achievement based" (i.e. that they must state what learners *will have done* in

---

7. Vella originally identified "seven steps of planning" (Vella, *Taking Learning to Task*, 24–25). Recently, Global Learning Partners has extended these to eight. For the eight-step process, see "The 8 Steps of Design," Global Learning Partners, accessed 21 September 2017, http://www. globallearningpartners.com/about/about-dialogue-education/the-8-steps-of-design. We have taken the liberty of placing the additional step later in the sequence than it is placed in the Global Learning Partners revision. We believe this is consistent with Vella's original intent.

order to assure themselves and others that they have learned). Here, again, Vella gives practical expression to Freire's call for praxis learning. Historically, teaching objectives have addressed what teachers will do and learning objectives have described what learners "will be able to do." Vella argues that learning objectives are "soft," that they allow teachers to feel they have done their part when they have taught a lesson, without verifying that learners are able to apply what has been taught.

"Achievement-based objectives" state learning in active terms. Thus, when the teaching–learning experience is complete, both teachers and learners "know they know" because learners have demonstrated their learning. Well-crafted achievement-based objectives will imply the teaching–learning method to be used, Vella's "How?"

Both Freire and Vella have much to contribute to those involved in ministry education. Freire's metaphor of a "banking" approach, so common in traditional education, provides valuable insight into the incapacity of this approach to affect true transformation. "Banking" education is a deeply flawed approach for developing mature, competent, spiritual leaders for the church.

Freire's and Vella's observations regarding the "oppressive" nature of hierarchical approaches to teaching and the value and importance of mutual respect in teacher–learner relationships are worthy of consideration and biblical reflection. While the Bible clearly affirms the role of teacher, Jesus also made clear the posture teachers should assume. He said, "You are not to be called rabbi [i.e. teacher], for you have one teacher, and you are all brothers . . . Neither be called instructors, for you have one instructor, the Christ" (Matt 23:8, 10). When we allocate authority to ourselves or exercise power in relation to our learners, we violate Christ's example and command. The inappropriateness of hierarchical posturing is especially stark when we lead the divinely called and gifted adult learners our seminaries enroll.

Freire's denunciation of "oppressive" modes of teaching and his advocacy of inviting learners into dialogue may raise unnecessary concerns.[8] In doing

---

8. In Western cultures, and diffused internationally through cultural globalization, many educators have embraced a constructivist epistemology that affirms multiple truths and denies the need or possibility of testing truth claims. Such assumptions are problematic, both philosophically and biblically. While it is self-evident that learning develops through experience, direct and mediated, our understandings and truth claims can and must be tested. Everyone must live in the world God has created and everyone is accountable to the theological and moral

so, Freire does not diminish the role of the teacher. Both in his writing and in Vella's, the teaching–learning process is managed by the teacher. When Freire and his team entered a village they already had a teaching–learning goal, the conscientization of the people. Furthermore, they did not consult the people regarding framing "generative themes" or methods to be used; those were determined by the teaching team. Their process is dialogical and interactive but responsibility for the teaching–learning outcome rested on the teaching team. The same is true with Vella. It is the teacher who works through the "eight steps of planning" and directs the teaching–learning interaction. The language, at times, may appear exclusively egalitarian but the reality never diminishes the role or responsibility of the teacher. The call for egalitarian postures is presented in contrast to the oppressive postures typical of "banking" education common in Freire's post-colonial Brazil and on too many university and seminary campuses today.

Freire's and Vella's emphasis on the interactive role of knowing and doing cannot be overemphasized. Ministry preparation must, by necessity, involve reflection in the context of action and action in the context of reflection. While many seminaries and Bible colleges have sought to address this aspect of dialogic learning (at least superficially) through field education, few have incorporated these reflection and action elements in course and lesson design. Ministry education's capacity to transform can be greatly enhanced as we learn to identify with our learners, design curricula that address their real needs, and engage them through respectful, authentic dialogue.

---

truth God has revealed. If I construct a view of the world that is at odds with the world God has created (e.g. I believe I can walk through walls), I will get bruised. Similarly, if I construct theological or moral perspectives that are at odds with God's revelation in the Scriptures, I will face him as my judge. It is our fallen drive to escape God's judgment, to realize a godless autonomy, that underlies relativistic constructivism. Some who advocate for learner-centered education, embracing this relativistic constructivism, view students as self-validating truth-makers rather than as truth-learners. Other advocates for learner-centered education appeal to principles that avoid these problems and are open to critical validation. Maryellen Weimer's helpful book, *Learner-Centered Teaching* (San Francisco: Jossey-Bass, 2002), is an example of positive learner-centeredness.

Bloom: A Taxonomy of Cognitive Functions

In 1949, Benjamin Bloom, Associate Director of the University of Chicago's Board of Examinations, initiated a multi-institutional project designed to enable universities and faculty members to share examination questions. In the late 1940s, behavioristic psychology[9] reigned in university circles and Tyler's four-step approach to curriculum development[10] was widely embraced. Both assigned high value to clearly specified learning objectives. This was the context in which Bloom launched his project.

The first step for Bloom and his colleagues was to distinguish three "domains" of learning: the "cognitive domain" (i.e. learning related to knowing and reasoning), the "affective domain" (i.e. learning related to emotions and feeling), and the "psychomotor domain" (i.e. learning related to actions and behaviors). In 1956, Bloom and his colleagues published *Taxonomy of Educational Objectives: Volume 1, The Cognitive Domain*, followed eight years later by *Volume 2, The Affective Domain*.[11] Although Bloom's taxonomy of cognitive processes did not facilitate exchange of examination items, as originally hoped, it has enjoyed wide acceptance as a schema for designing and clarifying instructional objectives.

The six cognitive processes identified are: Remembering, Understanding, Applying, Analyzing, Evaluating, and Creating. These functions typically are arrayed as a hierarchy, as in Figure 3.1.

---

9. See B. F. Skinner, *Science and Human Behavior* (New York: Free Press, 1953).

10. See Ralph W. Tyler, *Basic Principles of Curriculum and Instruction* (Chicago: University of Chicago Press, 1949).

11. Both volumes were published by Longman Publishing Group, New York. Volume 2, with its proposed taxonomy of affective objectives, is rarely cited and the original team did not publish a taxonomy of "psychomotor" functions. In 2001, David Krathwohl, a member of the original team, collaborated in an "update" of the original taxonomy of cognitive functions. Rather than a simple hierarchy, as the original taxonomy, the revised taxonomy is a four-by-six matrix with four "dimensions" of knowledge on the vertical axis and the original six cognitive "processes," renamed and slightly reordered, on the horizontal axis (David R. Krathwohl, "A Revision of Bloom's Taxonomy: An Overview," *Theory into Practice* 41, no. 4 [Autumn 2002]: 215–218). The hierarchy presented here is the original, with the names and order of the revised taxonomy.

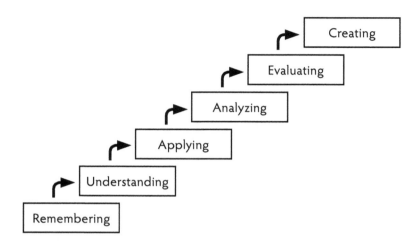

Figure 3.1: Bloom's Taxonomy of Cognitive Processes

"Remembering" is the simplest cognitive process. One does not manipulate the knowledge in view; it simply is retrieved from memory. "Understanding" refers to establishing the meaning of the knowledge retrieved, including communicating that meaning verbally or graphically. "Applying" refers to using the knowledge within a specific context. These three are often referred to as "lower order" cognitive functions, since they do not require reasoning.

"Higher order" cognitive functions include the three processes at the top of the hierarchy. "Analyzing" refers to deconstructing the remembered knowledge to identify assumptions and embedded data as well as locating the information with respect to other information, concepts, or schemata. More demanding is "Evaluating" (i.e. assessing the remembered knowledge using identifiable criteria and standards). The highest order of cognitive process, according to Bloom's taxonomy, is "Creating" (previously termed "Synthesis"), that is, manipulating the remembered knowledge or combining it with other knowledge to produce new perspectives or insights.

One of the significant benefits of Bloom's taxonomy has been recognition by teaching faculty that instruction and assessment have often been directed toward the "lower order" cognitive processes. This has stimulated interest in developing students' "higher order" processes and in exploring methods of instruction that model and demand analysis, evaluation, and creative synthesis. Because God has communicated truth verbally and rationally, it is important for seminaries to develop the higher-order thinking skills of candidates for ministry in the church and community. Traditional approaches to seminary education, with instructional objectives and teaching methods that almost exclusively focus on remembering and reproducing, fall short of this goal. Careful attention to Bloom's taxonomy can be both challenging and helpful as we seek to fulfill our responsibility to develop the minds of our students.

Brain-Imaging Technology: The Physiology of Learning

Recent developments in brain-imaging technology have allowed scientists literally to observe the brain at work.[12] As subjects are given different stimuli or tasks, neurobiologists can locate quite specifically the areas of the brain that are most active under particular stimuli. This capability has greatly advanced our understanding of the human brain, with significant benefit for educators. It validates some approaches to teaching and learning while discrediting others.

The human brain may be described as consisting of two major regions. The first is the cerebral cortex, which is the place where conscious thought occurs. The second is the sub-cortical region, or the "deep brain." The autonomic (i.e. involuntary and unconscious) and emotional functions of the brain are centered in the deep brain. The cerebral cortex has been described as "a thick bark" that overlies the deep brain.

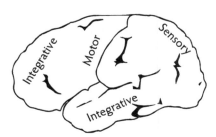

Figure 3.2: The Cerebral Cortex[13]

---

12. A helpful resource on the biology of learning is James E. Zull, *The Art of Changing the Brain: Enriching the Practice of Teaching by Exploring the Biology of Learning* (Sterling, VA: Stylus, 2002).

13. Reprinted from Zull, *Art of Changing the Brain*, 15, with permission of the publisher. Copyright © 2002, Stylus Publishing, LLC.

In Figure 3.2 the cerebral cortex is depicted, with the front of the brain at the left. It shows three functions related to learning and the approximate center of each. Note that there are two "integrative" regions of the cortex. The integrative region at the back of the brain is the "temporal integrative cortex" and that at the front of the brain is the "frontal integrative cortex." As sensory data are received, these areas of the brain normally interact to establish meaning and response in the following cyclical pattern:

1. *Sensory:* Signals are received from the sense organs – eyes, ears, skin, mouth, and nose.
2. *Temporal Integrative Cortex:* Sensory data are integrated to produce meaning as signals are added to existing concepts (cf. Piaget's *assimilation*) or combined into new units that expand conceptual understanding (cf. Piaget's *accommodation*). The temporal integrative cortex also is the depository of short-term memory.
3. *Frontal Integrative Cortex:* Information from the back brain is integrated to form hypotheses or action plans that utilize or test concepts.
4. *Motor:* Signals are sent that effect physical or verbal actions implementing the formulated action plans.

The brain's functions normally follow this cycle, but progress is not always sequential; thought can trigger signals that bounce back and forth between the meaning-making (temporal integrative cortex) and planning or hypothesizing (frontal integrative cortex) regions of the brain. Information is formed into a hypothesis, which reminds us of different information, which then implies an alternative hypothesis, and so on. Thus, alternative plans or hypotheses are weighed until we elect one to express or test. This process of thought – reflecting and hypothesizing – is "hard-wired" into the brain as multiple bundles of nerves that connect the temporal integrative cortex and the frontal integrative cortex. Note how the structure and function of the brain supports Piaget's concept of disequilibration and Freire's and Vella's suggestion that effective learning experiences involve critical reflection in the context of action.

Although conscious thought is a function of the cerebral cortex, teachers also benefit from knowing a bit about the deep brain. The functions of the deep brain include the body's control center (e.g. heartbeat, breathing, and all the body's functions we normally don't think about), the function we commonly refer to as reflexes, and – more consequential for teaching and learning – long-term memory. Information closely related to personal survival or to our core values (shaped by worldview, culture, and relationships, including our family upbringing) are stored in long-term memory. For information to be transferred from short-term memory, in the temporal integrative cortex, to long-term memory, therefore, it is necessary for the information to be recognized as useful and valued.

Within the deep brain are two centers (one on each side) that constantly scan sensory data and filter it for indications of danger. These centers can send signals directly to the action region of the cerebral cortex. The result is often referred to as reflexes. Have you had the experience of having a bug fly into your eyelid? The reason the bug hit your eyelid instead of flying into your eye is because these sensors in your deep brain recognized the threat posed by the bug and commanded your eye to close without waiting for you to think about it. These centers also trigger our sensation of fear. Just as they bypass rational processes when sensing threat, they can shut down rational processes when fear becomes significant. This is why some students experience a "mental block" when taking examinations.

Interestingly, although the fear centers are located in the deep brain, pleasure centers are located in the cerebral cortex, in proximity to the frontal integrative cortex where choices and planning occur. When we experience something pleasurable, our natural response is, "Ooo, I like that! How can I get more of it?" Pleasure isn't only physical; it also comes from positive relationships, experiences of success, and affirmation by others whom we respect. Understanding basic facts about the emotional centers of the brain can help teachers know how to motivate and help their students.

Zull points out that experience is changed, or "transformed," as the brain converts experience into understanding. He notes three specific transformations:[14]

1. *Past to future:* As the brain processes information, reflection on assimilated concepts (past) yields new thoughts (future). Similarly, past experience becomes plans for future action.

---

14. Zull, 33–34.

2. *External to internal:* External stimuli become internal understandings.
3. *Controlled to controlling:* As understanding develops, an individual exchanges dependent reaction to his or her environment for empowered action and ability to shape that environment.

Unlike the theorists discussed in this chapter, the findings of brain-imaging research do not present an integrative picture of transformational education. What they do provide is evidence of the way God has structured the human brain. Nevertheless, brain research appears to support Piaget's thesis that the learner is an active agent, a producer of knowledge, rather than merely a passive receptor. Brain research also supports Freire's and Vella's emphasis on the value of education as dialogue, the need and capacity for conscientization, and the essential role of praxis in education that transforms. Careful reflection will reveal other implications for educational theory and practice.

Kolb: The Cycle of Learning

David Kolb, a contemporary American adult educator, builds on learning theories developed by John Dewey and Jean Piaget to suggest that learning progresses in a circular pattern; he refers to this pattern as "the learning cycle" (see Figure 3.3).[15] According to Kolb, learning begins with *concrete experience* – physical, aural, or visual, from our environment, or verbal, through conversation or reading. The entry points are our five sense organs: eyes, ears, nose, mouth, and skin.

The next step in the learning cycle is *reflective observation.* We organize sensory data, attempt to make meaning from it, and locate it with respect to prior experience. It is at this point that we might say we "understand" what we have experienced.

As learning progresses and we reflect on the meaning of our experience, we explore its implications: we build *abstract hypotheses* about the way this bit of understanding may relate to the rest of what we "know" and we plan ways to use or test our understanding.

The fourth step in Kolb's learning cycle is *active testing.* We may not think of "testing" our understanding in any kind of controlled way, but by using it, we

---

15. D. A. Kolb, *Experiential Learning* (Englewood Cliffs, NJ: Prentice Hall, 1984).

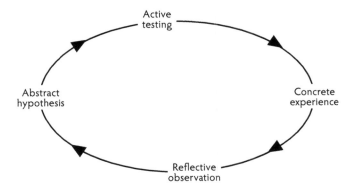

Figure 3.3: Kolb's Learning Cycle

throw our understandings against the hard realities of the world external to our minds. "Active testing" may take any of several forms. Simply expressing our understandings allows others to dispute or concur with our understandings. (Even talking to ourselves has some value in this regard.) Writing down our understandings is a physical and mental discipline that externalizes thoughts. Of course, when we act on our ideas, we test them, as well.

Note that when we act on our understandings, we generate new "concrete experience," which must be interpreted, challenging or reinforcing our prior understandings, and suggesting new ways to use our modified or confirmed understandings, which then also must be tested. And so the learning cycle continues. The learning cycle may be interrupted at any point, of course. When that happens, learning stalls or ceases.

Kolb's learning cycle suggests that there are *natural polarities* involved in the learning process: *concrete/abstract* and *reflective/active* (see Figure 3.4). No one person is equally good at everything; some excel at concrete thinking while others handle abstractions better. Some enjoy reflecting, while others want to be active – even to the point of skipping careful planning (the abstract phase) and plunging directly into acting on ideas in the old "trial and error" pattern. Do you recognize your own learning tendencies relative to these categories?

Recognizing that these differences exist can be important to the teacher since they suggest different learners will bring different preferences and strengths to the learning experience. The teacher will need to design learning opportunities that take into account the different strengths individuals bring

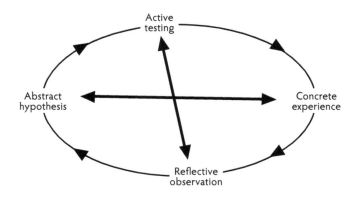

Figure 3.4: Polarities in Kolb's Learning Cycle

to the experiences of learning. At the same time, learning activities should encourage learners to engage each step of the learning cycle.

You may have recognized that there is notable consistency between Kolb's learning cycle and what brain science has discovered about the brain and learning. Zull notes this, as well.[16] When we compare what we know about the brain with Kolb's learning cycle, we see interesting correlations (see Figure 3.5).

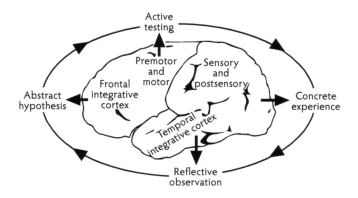

Figure 3.5: Kolb's Learning Cycle and Functions of the Brain[17]

16. Zull, *Art of Changing the Brain*, 18–19.

17. Reprinted from Zull, *Art of Changing the Brain*, 18, with permission of the publisher. Copyright © 2002, Stylus Publishing, LLC.

We even may conclude that recent advances in brain-imaging technology confirm Kolb's theories. In a sense, the learning cycle is "hard-wired" into the structure of the brain. Kolb didn't invent it; he just articulated how the brain processes data as it converts stimuli into learning.

Mezirow: Transformative Learning

Both the title and the intent of this book imply that ministry education should go beyond producing knowledgeable graduates. Its aim, instead, should be transformation in the lives and minds of learners. Recognition that learning experiences should result in significant change in learners is not limited to ministry education. As we have seen, this value has been central to each of the educational theorists considered in this chapter. Although they come from different perspectives and experiences, each believes that education should result in changed actions and behavior patterns resulting from new understandings and assumptions.

Jack Mezirow introduced the concept of "transformative learning" in a study of women who had returned to community college to continue their education after being out of school for an extended period.[18] He and his colleagues developed the concept as a theory for adult education. The initial study, as well as later research, identified *perspective transformation* as central to transformative learning. Perspective transformation goes beyond information processing and results in deep and lasting change in a learner's basic assumptions, beliefs, feelings, and behaviors.

Mezirow identified four elements as essential to transformative learning. As you consider the following elements, note the parallels and consistencies with the other theorists discussed in this chapter.

1. *Disorienting Dilemma:* Perspective transformation often is "triggered" by an event in an individual's life that has deep significance and that "typically exposes a discrepancy between what a person has always

---

18. Jack Mezirow, *Education for Perspective Transformation: Women's Re-Entry Programs in Community Colleges* (New York: Center for Adult Education, Teachers College, Columbia University, 1978).

assumed to be true and what has just been experienced, heard, or read."[19] The triggering episode could be a single event or a series of events. Mezirow points out that educational activities such as problem-solving provide an opportunity to highlight discrepancies between what learners assume to be true and what they experience in the activity.[20]

2. *Critical Reflection:* Transformative learning must involve a deliberate, systematic analysis, evaluation, and reassessment of one's basic assumptions, beliefs, feelings, and behaviors in light of new experience or knowledge. Mezirow insists that "by far the most significant learning experiences in adulthood involve critical reflection – reassessing the way we have posed problems and reassessing our own orientation to perceiving, knowing, believing, feeling, and acting."[21]

3. *Reflective Discourse:* For transformative learning to occur, individuals need to engage in dialogue or discourse with others. Mezirow suggests that "discourse is necessary to validate what and how one understands, or to arrive at a best judgment regarding a belief."[22] Recent research indicates an important relational dynamic to this discourse; it occurs only in a trusted community where individuals can safely question accepted beliefs, attitudes, assumptions, and norms.[23]

4. *Learner Autonomy:* Mezirow sets the previous two elements (critical thinking and reflective discourse) in the context of learner autonomy or self-directed learning.

> In fostering self-direction, the emphasis is on creating an environment in which learners become increasingly adept at learning from each other and at helping each other learn in problem-solving groups. The educator functions

---

19. Patricia Cranton, "Teaching for Transformation," *New Directions for Adult and Continuing Education* 2002, no. 93 (2002): 63–72.

20. Jack Mezirow, "Transformative Learning: Theory to Practice," *New Directions for Adult and Continuing Education* 1997, no. 74 (1997): 5–12.

21. Jack Mezirow, *Fostering Critical Reflection in Adulthood: A Guide to Transformative and Emancipatory Learning* (San Francisco: Jossey-Bass, 1990), 13.

22. Mezirow, "Transformative Learning," 10.

23. Edward W. Taylor, "Analyzing Research on Transformational Learning Theory," in Jack Mezirow and Associates, *Learning as Transformation: Critical Perspectives on a Theory in Progress,* 1st ed. (San Francisco: Jossey-Bass, 2000), 285–328.

as a facilitator and provocateur rather than as an authority on subject matter.[24]

Cranton also noted Mezirow's emphasis on "shifting expertise, power, and decision-making" from the educator to the learner in the process of transformative learning.[25]

Transformative learning theory, as it has developed over the last several decades, builds upon and utilizes the essential elements of other learning theories mentioned in this chapter. It is a valuable tool, a topic worthy of further study by those engaged in educational endeavors, such as ministry education, that are intended to transform lives.

In Mezirow's approach to transformational education, the goal of the educator is to evoke change in perspective. Within a Christian framework, this understanding of transformation is conflicted. The appropriateness of and need for altered perspectives is very clear but the Christian needs to say much more. Unstated (but assumed) in Mezirow's writings are assumptions and values toward which Mezirow believes the learner should progress, such as value relativism and individual autonomy, grounded in a constructivist epistemology. As respected persons, the perspectives of teachers exert significant influence toward shaping the thinking of students. In academic environments, reigning perspectives often differ markedly from biblical truth and values. While perspective transformation can dramatically affect one's values and behaviors, true transformation occurs only as learners' lives are aligned with that of Jesus Christ and the truth of God's Word.

Conclusion

In light of the principles considered in this chapter and a biblical understanding of God's work among his people, we suggest that education becomes transformational when an institution or a teacher creates an environment – through personal modeling, through curricular and course design, and through

---

24. Mezirow, "Transformative Learning," 11.
25. Patricia Cranton, "Self-Directed and Transformational Instructional Development," *Journal of Higher Education* 65, no. 6 (1994): 726–744.

in-class and out-of-class interaction – that encourages learners to integrate God's truth into their fundamental perspectives, core values, relational patterns, and habits of life, thereby opening themselves to God's transforming power. When learners are transformed by God's grace, this transformation impacts every aspect of life and is lived out in community.[26]

A commitment to engaging in ministry education that transforms rather than just informs, therefore, may require teachers to confront their own need for "perspective transformation." For many ministry educators, basic assumptions, values, beliefs, and actions concerning the practice of valid ministry education need to be reassessed in light of the research, theories, and findings reviewed in this chapter.

Do our educational activities include moments of "disequilibrium" or "disorienting dilemmas" that afford learners opportunity to re-examine old ideas and assumptions in light of new truth or experience? To what extent do we use dialogue to gain insight into learners' current perspectives, ideas, and even misunderstandings concerning a given topic? Is that discourse provided in an egalitarian, "safe," and reflective manner? Are we engaging learners in a full-orbed learning cycle that fully utilizes the brain's innate capabilities to assimilate new information in ways that empower action and shape context? Although biblical and theological content is essential to ministry preparation, it is equally essential that learners engage that content in ways that transform both life and ministry potential.

---

26. The proposed definition of transformational education was developed by the GATE team and can be found on the GATE website. See www.gateglobal.org/about.html.

4

Teaching for Transformation: From Theory to Practice

The previous chapter noted areas of educational research and learning theory that have relevance to ministry education that transforms. Nothing is more practical than good theory but good theory must be put into practice. The research and theory reported in chapter 3 can inform the ways we plan and teach.

Contexts That Shape Educational Encounters

In chapter 3, we noted Vella's "eight steps of planning" and observed that the order of the steps is important. Rather than beginning by asking "What will I teach?," Vella observes that several steps are needed before we can address that question appropriately. We refer to Vella's first four steps as "antecedents" to course or curricular planning.

Vella's first step is to ask, *"Who?"* Before we can plan a course or curriculum we need to learn what we can about the learners we will teach. Learners bring both needs and resources into our classrooms. Not only their prior schooling is relevant. It also is important to learn all we can about their spiritual experience and maturity, their family, their cultural background, the stresses they face which could impact their studies, and the hurdles they have overcome in order to study with us. Teachers of advanced courses can get to know students who already are enrolled on their campus but addressing the "Who?" is more challenging for teachers of first-year courses or in off-campus workshops. If application forms are designed to gather information useful to teachers, those can be available for review by teachers when planning syllabi. Some teachers may want to interview prospective students by telephone or request students to post to a secure website a brief self-introduction that includes information relevant to their course. The more we know about learners who will enroll in our courses, the more appropriately we can design our instruction. If nothing else, the first day of class can include a "Getting to Know You" questionnaire that elicits information relevant to the course. Vella terms such an exercise a learner needs and resources assessment.[1]

Knowledge about our students can help us decide what we need to teach and what we do not need to teach based on what learners already know. It can help us address issues that are relevant to their environments, their backgrounds, and their probable places of future ministry. Understanding the spiritual maturity of students and their prior experience in church and ministry alerts us to opportunities to draw them into dialogue and to build on their experience as a resource for their own learning and for the learning of others in the class.

Vella advises that a second antecedent question for teachers is *"Why?"* This is not "Why am I teaching this course?" or "Why is this course included in our school's curriculum?" Those are important questions in other contexts since they explore our personal calling and the rationale that supports our school's programs. When planning a course or curriculum, however, we also need to ask, "Why do my adult students come to our school, or to this course?" What is their motivation? What do they expect to learn? How do they hope to use the knowledge they develop? How and in what ways do they want to grow and change – intellectually, spiritually, and professionally – as a result of their experience in this course?

Understanding student motivations and goals enables us to plan learning experiences that appeal to their interests and that are relevant to their calling and ministry contexts. In order to learn, students must be engaged. When we plan our curricula, courses, and lessons with students' motivations in mind, we are better able to engage them in the learning process.

---

1. Jane Vella, *On Teaching and Learning* (San Francisco: Jossey-Bass, 2008), 19–29.

A third antecedent question is *"When?"* This is not limited to the time of day, although that may be important to planning. Late-night classes or classes scheduled after the noon meal, in the heat of the day when focused attention is more challenging, may need to be planned differently from classes scheduled at the beginning of the day. Just as important, however, is the course schedule. Is this an intensive course that meets daily for one or two weeks, perhaps during the rainy season or in the winter? Is it a weekend course that meets monthly on Friday afternoon through Saturday afternoon? Is it a course that meets once, twice, or three times a week over the length of a term? If so, how long is the term? Four weeks? Six weeks? Ten weeks? Fifteen weeks? What vacations and holidays are scheduled during this term? All of these questions bear on the design of a course. Similar considerations bear on the design of curricula and lessons.

When planning begins without giving appropriate attention to the "When?," we tend to include more content in our classes than is realistic. We then feel rushed and revert to lecturing, even though we may recognize that student learning suffers. An axiom of adult education is "Less is more." That is not a limitless rule, of course, but it is a helpful reminder that our tendency to include more and more content in our lessons actually inhibits student learning. When we focus on what is essential and allow students time to process and reflect on the principles and truths taught, learning increases. This principle is more demanding of the teacher, since we must understand so thoroughly the topics we teach that we can identify and help learners understand the core information, concepts, and relationships. By teaching our learners where and how to access additional learning resources, we equip them for life-long learning. Personal illustrations make learning meaningful; time must be allowed for this kind of sharing. This is our calling and our privilege. By being selective in the amount of information we transfer and by focusing on student engagement with the central truths and principles we teach, learning in our classes becomes transformative.

It also is important for educational planners to consider *"Where?"* This includes not only the location and physical space provided for learning, but also the configuration of the room, facilities and equipment available to support the teaching–learning process, as well as resources available in the broader community.

The most common classroom arrangement places students in rows, all facing the front of the room where the teacher stands or is seated, facing the class. The implicit message is clear: All that is important happens at the front of the room. The teacher's role is central to learning. Since students are not expected to contribute much of significance, it is appropriate for students to view only the back of their peers' heads.

Each of these assumptions is problematic when we are committed to ministry education that transforms. As Vella reminds us, adult teaching and learning is a collaborative endeavor that proceeds best through dialogue. The most natural context for collaborative dialogue in most cultures is a circle, often seated around a table. When lesson plans include learning tasks, it is appropriate to choose a classroom provided with tables at which students work in small groups of four to six. Placing students in table groups implicitly communicates that what happens at the tables is important. The teacher's role still is critically important since it is his or her responsibility to provide the direction and resources students need to complete the assigned tasks. The table group, however, is where learning occurs. A learning space that lacks the flexibility required to place students in table groups is not an insurmountable obstacle to dialogic teaching and learning. Nevertheless, such spaces demand more creative planning and instructional management.

Planning also must take into consideration the facilities and equipment available to support teaching and learning. If work done in table groups is to be posted, for example, rooms that have large windows and a natural airflow may require different planning from those that have large walls and are climate-controlled. When preparing handouts, photocopy services that are available only at an off-campus copy shop place demands on planning that are different from those of photocopy services available on campus. Teaching activities that require a video projector, a computer, or a DVD player will be useable in some classrooms but not in others.

Furthermore, learning need not be limited to the classroom. When planning courses and lessons, teachers should consider resources and opportunities available in the larger community. Local pastors and Christian leaders may be invited to share their experience and insights with students, either in the classroom or (better!) in their places of ministry. Students gain ministry experience as well as opportunities to apply learning when they engage in service or evangelistic projects in the community outside the campus. Some schools include in their curricula scheduled periods when students and faculty, together, engage in week-long ministry.

Vella's first four "steps of planning," what we have termed the antecedent questions, prepare us to design curricula and to determine the content for our courses and lessons that are most appropriate for and most relevant to the context and calling of our students. They enable us to engage our students in learning that truly is transformational.

The Role of Prior Experience in Learning

Brain-imaging technology has confirmed what educators have always known but often neglect: New learning must build on existing knowledge or experience. What neuroscientists have learned about the function of the brain can help us teach more effectively.

The brain is made up of special cells, known as "neurons." Each of these special cells conveys information to other cells. The junctures between cells through which signals pass are called "synapses." The cerebral cortex is made up of (literally!) billions of these special cells that communicate in established patterns.[2] Through multiple synapses, these cells establish networks in which meaning is formed and memories are stored. Everything we know exists in the form of these networks. Even newborn babies have established networks. These networks are physical and persistent. Learning entails building new connections from already existing ones. New neuronal networks are formed and learning occurs only as new experiences are linked to concepts, memories, and experiences already stored in the brain.

The findings of neuroscience confirm that learning must begin from what already is known. Knowing our learners and connecting the truths we teach to their prior knowledge and experience is essential to helping them learn. Our adult learners bring to our classes a wealth of prior knowledge and experience. With billions of neurons networked in each learner's brain, our students possess unimaginable potential for learning. Teachers who relate new truths or skills to

---

2. James E. Zull, *The Art of Changing the Brain: Enriching the Practice of Teaching by Exploring the Biology of Learning* (Sterling, VA: Stylus, 2002), 97.

prior knowledge have a lot to work with! When students "don't understand," it is because we have yet to connect the truths we teach to the prior knowledge of our students.

Effective Lectures

Because educators commend interactive methods of teaching, it is sometimes assumed they are dismissive of lecturing. Although some may be guilty of undervaluing the lecture method, in fact there are several situations in which lecturing is the best way to achieve our educational goals. Examples include when introducing unfamiliar theory, when explaining complex concepts, when stimulating interest in a new topic, or when modeling intellectual inquiry. A focused lecture may also be the best way to assure that learners have all the information needed to address a learning task.

Assumptions Inherent in Lecturing

Lectures are a valuable educational method but they do entail several assumptions that must be recognized.[3] First, when we lecture we assume that learners prefer, or at least are proficient in, the auditory learning style. One need not endorse a particular theory of learning styles to recognize that some individuals and cultures prefer more visual modes of communication while others prefer verbal or aural communication. Students who prefer visual communication easily get lost when communication – especially complex or technical communication – is restricted to verbal channels. These students are disadvantaged when lecture is the dominant method of instruction.

Second, when we lecture we assume that learners lack access to alternative means of acquiring the content lectured. There may have been a time when that generally was true but students today have available many resources if they are taught to access them. Faculty members typically have a broader grasp of data related to their discipline fields and a deeper understanding of relationships existing within the field. Wisdom is needed to discern when and

---

3. A helpful discussion of assumptions inherent in lecturing can be found in D. W. Johnson, R. T. Johnson, and K. A. Smith, *Active Learning: Cooperation in the College Classroom* (Edina, MN: Interaction Book Company, 2006), 5:01–5:09.

how to share this advanced understanding. Nevertheless, the value of guided self-discovery is fundamental to teaching and learning. Teachers who lecture everything develop dependent learners.

Third, when we lecture we assume that learners have mastered knowledge on which the current lecture builds. A student who lacks specific information, experience, or theoretical structures needed to comprehend the subject of a lecture can quickly become lost and disengage from the learning experience. Of course, this is true when knowledge is gained through other means as well, but a student who is reading or engaged in discovery learning can pause to acquire the needed background before proceeding. This is not possible when attending a lecture.

Fourth, when we lecture we assume that learners have good note-taking strategies and skills. Identifying critically important concepts and information within a flood of words is a demanding task that assumes a framework for filtering what is heard. Students who lack the needed frameworks or skill in applying them tend to assume everything included in a lecture is equally important. This leads them to attempt to take notes as dictation and to memorize all that is lectured. Storing meaningless words in short-term memory is not a useful form of learning. Unless a school's curriculum includes guidance on note-taking, the usefulness of student notes typically varies widely across a lecture class.

Fifth, when we lecture we assume that learners are not susceptible to information-processing overload. Because the content of the lecture is familiar to the teacher, it is easy to overlook the complexity and broader theoretical context of the material lectured. When the lecturer's progress outpaces the capacity of learners, learners disengage and learning ceases. This problem, as with other assumptions inherent in lectures, can be mitigated to some extent by allowing opportunities for students to reflect and to raise questions. A teacher's commitment to "cover the content," combined with the admirable desire to share as much as possible of his or her own understanding, can, however, lead to non-stop lecturing, learner overload, and cessation of learning.

Qualities of Effective Lectures

Lecturing can be an excellent method to promote learning, provided the method is not overused. Effective lectures relate new information to prior knowledge, engage students' emotions, and employ a variety of cognitive activities.

The findings of brain research reviewed in the previous chapter indicate that new neuronal networks are developed from established networks. Lecturers do well, therefore, to identify linkages between new information or concepts and that already known. Furthermore, since thinking proceeds from the concrete to the abstract (as noted by Kolb), lectures that include concrete examples will aid student comprehension.

Comprehension also improves when lecturers clearly state the purpose and central ideas of their lecture. Brookfield even suggests distribution of "scaffolding notes," an abbreviated outline of the lecture that "give[s] enough information so that students can follow the lecture's progress" but not so much as to relieve the student of need to be present and attentive.[4] Similarly, it is helpful to identify digressions and illustrations so students are not confused.

Effective lectures not only build on established knowledge, they also gently challenge student perceptions and assumptions with new information, concepts, and perspectives. As we saw in the previous chapter, both Piaget and Mezirow noted the central role of disequilibration in transformative learning.

Brain research also validates the importance of engaging student emotions to increase learning. When learners see that a lecturer values a topic, their interest is piqued as well. This does not mean that every lecture should march from one emotional high to another, but students are more likely to embrace and retain information and insights when lecturers are passionate about the subjects they teach.

Stories often are an effective way to engage students' emotions. Stories may illustrate the importance or application of the information shared. Personal examples of discovery or application are particularly effective, since they make the connection between the subject matter and the person of the lecturer. Transparency is attractive in the classroom, as in all human relationships.

Finally, effective lectures employ a variety of cognitive skills. Brookfield cites Bligh's research to suggest "approximately twelve minutes as the optimum

---

4. Stephen D. Brookfield, *The Skillful Teacher*, 2nd ed. (San Francisco: Jossey-Bass, 2006), 107.

period of time in which students can be expected to focus on one idea or subtheme."[5] To retain student attention and engagement, lecturers can employ both linear and "looping" logic. "Looping logic" observes a concept from various perspectives, each "loop" returning to the central fact or concept to be established. Thus, a concept like the Trinity may be approached biblically, historically, devotionally, and practically, each loop returning to the observation that this doctrine is central to biblical Christianity.

In light of the transient nature of focus, noted by Bligh, Brookfield suggests "chunking" lectures (i.e. dividing lecture time into twelve-to-fifteen-minute segments separated by other learning activities). A thoughtful question on the topic just lectured with a couple minutes of silent reflection or writing can elicit productive thought and reignite student interest and engagement. Students may be given opportunity to express their observations or additional questions, or may be clustered in twos or threes for "buzz group" discussion of the question posed. Vella's advocacy of "learning tasks" begins with the observation that learners must have all the resources needed to accomplish the task assigned. Sometimes, a brief lecture is the best method of assuring that learners have the needed resources.

Lectures can be mind-numbing "teacher talk" or an effective method for promoting learning. The difference depends on how frequently the lecture method is used, how briefly it is used, and how effectively it is used. Wise teachers recognize lecturing as one method among others, best used in short segments, linking new learning to prior knowledge, and engaging students' emotions as well as their minds.

Leading Discussions and Debriefing Learning

Discussion is perhaps the most common alternative method to the lecture. Experiential learning and learning tasks must be debriefed to maximize learning, and debriefing typically takes the form of guided discussion. Insightful classroom discussions may occur serendipitously but most often they result from careful forethought and wise direction by the teacher.

---

5. Brookfield, *Skillful Teacher*, 105.

The Role of the Facilitator

As teachers, we have been socialized to think of teaching as talking – organizing and sharing information – rather than as facilitating learning. As we have seen, facilitating learning entails engaging the learner. Guided discussion is an effective way to engage learners and to facilitate learning.

For discussion or debriefing to be instructive, the facilitator must have a clear understanding of the learning goal. Common goals may be (1) to expose and test assumptions, (2) to clarify issues, (3) to explore application of principles, or (4) to extract general principles from particular experiences. When the goal of discussion is to explore application of principles, we assume that adult learners know their own context, so any reasonable suggestion may be affirmed. When the goal of discussion is to expose and test assumptions, to clarify issues, or to learn from particular experiences, the facilitator must be prepared to guide discussion. This will entail gently probing observations and assumptions while challenging those that appear to lack empirical or biblical support. Effective facilitators embrace their role with confidence but also with appropriate humility – we often learn from the insights of participants – and always with respect for others and their views. To do otherwise is to violate God's image in our learners.

Launching Discussions

Insightful discussion builds on shared experience, either direct (e.g. lecture, field experience, or simulation) or mediated (e.g. reading, case study, or video). The facilitator's role is to pose a question that engages participants and that provokes insight. The most helpful discussions are highly interactive but participants may need time to process a thoughtful question before responding.

Particularly at the launch of a discussion learners may be hesitant to be first to speak. As silence lengthens and tension grows, the facilitator faces the temptation to answer the question posed, but to do so almost always is a mistake. An effective facilitator will not be too quick to break the silence. Learners will not risk engaging questions if they realize the teacher will do it for them. If you realize your participants do not understand or misunderstand the point of a question, reframe it or state it in a different way. Instructive discussion or debriefing will begin when learners understand the question posed and recognize that you will not answer the question for them.

Responding to Participants

In any group discussion, volunteering an observation or suggestion entails a certain amount of risk. No one wants to be told they are wrong or to come away feeling foolish, sensing they missed important information that was clear to others. The courage exhibited by those who participate – especially those who are first to speak – deserves an expression of recognition and appreciation. Nevertheless, expressing appreciation does not require affirming every contribution. Indeed, universal affirmation confuses participants and does not contribute to building shared understandings. The teacher should have a goal in mind and should sensitively yet persistently guide discussion toward that goal.

Restating the contributions of participants wastes time and demeans the original contributor. It is not necessary for a facilitator to respond to every observation or suggestion offered. Sometimes thoughtful silence is the most effective response. At other times it is best to throw an observation back to the group. A facilitator may ask, "What do you think of that?" "How does that relate to the observation just made by Mary?"

Participant observations that are irrelevant or that move contrary to the goal of the discussion must be respectfully challenged by probing assumptions and perspectives that led to the observation shared. In doing this, we not only teach, we also model the higher-order thinking skills[6] we seek to develop in our learners. If an issue arises on which one or more participants take strong exception to the facilitator's perspective and instructional goal, it is appropriate to challenge the alternative view but it is not productive to engage in extended defense of one's own understanding. That always is a no-win scenario. Few participants will be persuaded by what appears to be an argument. The facilitator does better to ask one or two probing questions, then acknowledge that there may be room for further discussion and move on. This respects the dissenter, models humility, and trusts all participants to work through the issue for themselves.

---

6. Compare the section on Bloom's "Taxonomy of Cognitive Functions" in chapter 3.

Modeling and Experiential Learning

Demonstration is an important part of learning any skill and is a valuable aspect of character development. This is true of cognitive skills and ministry skills, just as it is of manual or artistic skills. As teachers, we model cognitive skills and we do well to be intentional in our modeling. In lectures and discussion, when we examine data, expose and test assumptions, and fairly present alternative interpretations, the process is as important as the goal.

After exposing previously unrecognized assumptions or deconstructing a specious argument, it is appropriate to say, "Did you see what I just did? Do you understand how I did it?" In other contexts, the question may be, "Did you observe how I responded to her?" "Was that an appropriate response? Why or why not?"

Students observe how we think and how we interact with others, whether present or absent. They also are quick to observe our integrity. Candor is respected. If an issue arises on which we have not formed an opinion, it is best to acknowledge we have more work to do. It also is appropriate, at times, to say, "I don't know" or "Let me think about that and get back to you." This is not permission to avoid the hard work of mastering one's discipline or thoughtfully preparing for interaction with students. When you've done your work and you encounter the unexpected, however, honesty is a better choice than pretense.

These principles are as valid for modeling spiritual submission to God's Word or ministry to others as for cognitive skills. When we teach the Bible, students recognize whether we approach it as a historical text to be analyzed or divine revelation to be obeyed. The Bible is a historical text and it is appropriate for us to subject it to careful exegesis. It never can be only a historical text, however. It always is God's truth that demands our humble obedience, that dictates our values and priorities, and that directs our relationships. When students observe our submission to the authority of God's Word and our commitment to obey it, they are shaped by our example.

The Elmers' Cycle of Learning

In light of the educational research and theory reviewed in chapter 3, Duane and Muriel Elmer have proposed a cycle of learning (see Figure 4.1) which

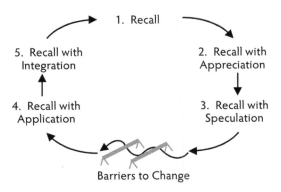

Figure 4.1: The Elmers' Cycle of Learning[7]

is most insightful.[8] There are several levels of learning that the theological educator must be aware of and pursue in teaching. Many teachers have a tendency to pursue only one level of learning at the expense of the others. This lopsided approach to learning has serious side effects. In fact, emphasizing *any one* of these at the expense of others will have negative consequences.

Level 1: Recall

The foundational level in teaching and learning is to teach for recall. To make a difference in their lives, our students need to be able to remember the truths we teach. Some educators who emphasize critical thinking skills speak poorly of teaching for recall but learners must first be able to remember the truth before they can understand it or use it. In anything we teach, we begin with what is known, whether we teach people to be airplane pilots, surgeons, or farmers.

To function effectively people must know relevant information. Level 1 addresses that concern in terms of the important information people must master to do a certain job. Mastery of information is only the beginning, however, and must never be seen as the end of education.

---

7. "Cycle of Learning" diagram ©1977, Duane H. Elmer and Muriel I. Elmer. Used by permission.

8. Duane H. Elmer and Muriel I. Elmer served on the education faculty of Trinity Evangelical Divinity School, Deerfield, IL, until their retirement in 2012. All material relating to the Cycle of Learning© is copyrighted by Duane H. and Muriel I. Elmer (unpublished paper, Michigan State University, 1977). The presentation here is used by permission of the authors.

In seminary education, Level 1 is an especially important starting point because God has given us divine revelation in the Holy Scripture. This means the truth we teach is authoritative and totally reliable. Jesus told the religious teachers of his day that they were wrong "because you know neither the Scriptures nor the power of God" (Matt 22:29). Their first problem was failure to recall, "to know," what God had taught in the Scriptures. The psalmist testifies, "I have stored up your word in my heart that I might not sin against you" (Ps 119:11). He recognizes that he must be able to recall God's Word if he is to benefit from it. In order to benefit from the truth we teach, our students must first be able to recall it.

Level 2: Recall with Appreciation

Recall of truth, however, is not the end of teaching or learning. Truth also must be valued. Many educators believe the "affective" part of learning may be the most important because it is a gateway to further learning. "Affect" has to do with affections: how we value and respond to a class, to information shared, to a teacher. The Bible calls this the heart response. Negative affect in a class closes the door to further learning. There may be a wide range of affective responses, or feelings, present in the classroom. Learners may exhibit interest, boredom, excitement, apathy, appreciation, or a range of other responses.

A critically important heart response is conviction, the work of the Holy Spirit as he shapes our affective response to the truth presented. Conviction is most powerful. We should study and teach in such a way that the Spirit of God can use his truth to convict us and our learners of things we are doing that are wrong ("sins of commission") and of things we are not doing but ought to be doing ("sins of omission").

When students leave our classroom with feelings of boredom, apathy, or frustration, the significance of the truth we teach may be lost. It is unlikely they will value that truth or do anything more with it. When they leave with feelings of interest, excitement, and appreciation, however, they are stimulated to pursue that truth, to reflect on it, and to obey it, even to share it with others.

Level 3: Recall with Speculation

As teachers, we want to move our students beyond appreciation; we want them to consider the significance of the truth they recall. We want to help them reflect, or "speculate." This level is called "speculation" to emphasize that we are not challenging learners to apply the truth we teach but only to think about applying it. This is something we can and should ask students to do in the classroom and in the work we assign.

When we think of speculation, we are asking the question, "So what?" If this truth were as important as it claims, what would be our appropriate response? What should I do about this information? What difference does it make that I have learned this truth? What adjustment or changes should it make in my life? My behavior? My relationships? The practice of my Christian faith?

Thinking about, or reflecting on, the truth we learn and recall is important. It enables us to plan wisely and to choose how we will respond. It also affords the Holy Spirit opportunity to guide our thoughts and to convict our hearts regarding our response to this truth. Paul prayed that the Christians in Colossae would "be filled with the knowledge of [God's] will . . . so as to walk in a manner worthy of the Lord, fully pleasing to him: bearing fruit in every good work and increasing in the knowledge of God" (Col 1:9–10). This level engages the will to change, to grow, to follow the Lord in obedience. As teachers, it is important for us to lead our students to this point of reflection, speculation, and decision.

Barriers to Change

Deciding to do something is the easy part. Since Satan does not want us to practice our Christian faith, he will try to prevent us from acting on the truth of Scripture. Jesus taught that it is "the evil one" who "snatches away what has been sown in [one's] heart" (Matt 13:19). Furthermore, there are things within us that hinder our making changes in our lives in accordance with God's Word (Rom 7:14–15). It is not enough to lead our learners to speculate about the application of God's truth; we also should challenge them to think about the barriers they may encounter as they begin to act on their decisions.

Barriers can take many forms. Fear is a common tactic of our enemy. "I've not done this before; maybe I can't do this!" "What if I try to apply this truth in my life, but fail?" The opinion of others is another powerful barrier many face. "Obedience to this truth is not common in my family or among my friends; what will they think of me?" "Will others laugh at me or reject me?" Busyness effectively prevents many from doing things they know they should. "I have so many other things I need to do before I can begin to act on the truth I know." We intend to apply God's truth in our lives but so often we never get around to doing it.

The more specifically we can identify the likely barriers we will encounter, the more helpfully we can plan to overcome them. Who is most likely to resist my doing as I have decided? Of whose disapproval am I most afraid? At what points am I most likely to encounter discouragement? This kind of thinking requires discipline but it can enable us to plan our responses and to follow through on our decisions to apply the truth we have learned.

Helping our learners identify potential barriers to applying God's truth is essential to developing strategies to overcome those barriers. Thus, identifying barriers is an extension of Level 3: "Recall with Speculation." We speculate first about our response to God's truth, then about barriers Satan may erect to deter us from obeying the truth, and, finally, how we can overcome those barriers. We decide what we need to do in response to the truth we have learned and we decide how we will respond when we encounter the barriers Satan is likely to throw in our path.

In most contexts, this is as far as we can lead our students in the classroom. The last two levels of learning must occur in the context of life.

Level 4: Recall with Application

This level of learning requires that students and teachers begin to apply some truth that God has made clear to us. It is a decision our students make as a result of what we helped them do in Level 3, including being realistic about the barriers and how to deal with them. It may entail reordered values and priorities, changed behavior, altered relationships, different patterns of response, or intentional choices to establish new habits. This is where truth impacts life. It is choosing to do what we know is right in light of the truth we know and recall. Thankfully, this is what God desires for us and what his grace enables.

The Scriptures are emphatic in calling us to obey the truth, to apply it in our lives. James repeatedly calls Christians to "be doers of the word [i.e. the message about God's truth], and not hearers only" (Jas 1:22–25; cf. 2:14–24; 3:13; 4:17). Peter taught that "obedience to the truth" purifies our souls (1 Pet 1:22); applying the truth cleanses us and prepares us to obey in other areas of life as well. John taught the importance of alignment between the Christian's verbal affirmations and life (1 John 3:18; cf. 1:5–7; 2:4–6; 2 John 4–6; 3 John 3–4). To know God's truth and to fail to apply it strips the truth of its power to transform our lives and effectively denies the truth we affirm.

Level 5: Recall with Integration

Integration is the ongoing practice of the truth so that it becomes a daily part of one's life. The truth that we disciplined ourselves to practice in Level 4 now has seamlessly woven itself into the fabric of our being: this is integrity. Our knowing and speaking truth becomes our living of truth. Our lives and our words communicate the same message. This is when truth becomes formative and transformative.

We cannot allow ourselves to be satisfied that students have learned until they have done something with the truth we have taught. We cannot assume that we have taught until there has been some life change in the people who have been in our classrooms.

There are many Scriptures that comment on loving God's truth, knowing it, "rightly handling" it (see 2 Tim 2:15), and protecting it. As we have seen, the Scriptures place knowing the truth and doing the truth together. In the Hebrew understanding of truth and life, the two are not separated. We do not know the truth until we have acted on it. Knowing and doing are assumed to be one.

Teaching for Transformation

In this chapter we have explored implications of the research findings and theories outlined in chapter 3. As our understanding grows regarding the way humans learn and the principles of teaching and learning, we are able to move beyond transferring information we have acquired and our understandings to our students. In place of only transferring information, we can begin to see the lives and ministries of our students transformed by the truth of God's Word and the power of his Spirit. We become partners with God in forming our students for transforming ministries in the places to which he calls them.

5

Modeling Transformative Leadership

Theological and educational foundations are invaluable guides when teaching for transformation of the lives and ministries of our students. They show us what to teach and how to teach. Even the best-designed educational process can be ineffective, however, if we ignore "The Luke 6:40 Principle." Luke records Jesus saying, "every one when he is fully taught will be like his teacher" (Luke 6:40 RSV). The success or failure of any educational project depends on the person of the teacher.[1] The teacher – not subject matter or methods – stands at the heart of the educational process. The effectiveness of the seminary depends on the lives, the hearts, the ministries, and the dedication of the faculty.

Jesus understood this. As we have seen, Jesus not only taught the importance of a life of faith, prayer, selfless love, and personal holiness, he also modeled these qualities. Jesus's harshest criticism was directed against religious conservatives of his day who held right theology but modeled insensitive, morally incongruent, legalistic leadership. He dismissed the Pharisees, saying, "you tithe mint and dill and cumin, and have neglected the weightier matters of the law: justice and mercy and faithfulness" (Matt 23:23). Twice Jesus reprimanded these leaders for their inverted values, charging them, "Go and learn what this means: 'I desire mercy, and not sacrifice'" (Matt 9:13; 12:7). The

---

1. A wonderful resource for personal reflection or faculty discussion on the person of the teacher is Parker Palmer's book, *The Courage to Teach: Exploring the Inner Landscape of a Teacher's Life* (San Francisco: Jossey-Bass, 1998).

problem of the Pharisees was not ignorance of God's law; they knew it well. Sadly, they did not model its core values.

Paul also understood the educational value of personal modeling. He was explicit with the church in Philippi, writing, "What you have learned and received and heard and seen in me – practice these things, and the God of peace will be with you" (Phil 4:9). To the church in Thessalonica he wrote, "you yourselves know how you ought to imitate us . . . [W]e worked night and day . . . to give you in ourselves an example to imitate" (2 Thess 3:7–9). To the Corinthian Christians he wrote, "Be imitators of me, as I am of Christ" (1 Cor 11:1).[2] Paul also urged Timothy (1 Tim 4:12) and Titus (Titus 2:7) to model the truths they taught.

The power of the life of the teacher in shaping the lives of students is demonstrable from our own experience, as well. If you think of the professor you most admired, you may recall only a few things that he or she said but you likely have no problem describing how his or her life touched yours.

The shaping effect of an example is not limited to the faculty, however; administrators and staff members also model values that students observe and from which they learn. A lecture on biblical servanthood can be greatly diminished, even nullified, by a student's encounter with a teacher, an administrator, a librarian, a registrar, a cook, or a gardener who is insensitive and demanding. It is essential, therefore, to reflect on the truths and values we intend to teach and to assess humbly our demonstration of those qualities.

Biblical Leadership Metaphors

When we look to Scripture for instruction on leadership we find three dominant metaphors. Leaders are portrayed as stewards, servants, and shepherds.[3]

---

2. On Paul's intentional modeling of the Christian life, see also Acts 20:35; 1 Cor 4:16; and Phil 3:17.

3. For an elaboration of these metaphors, see Ralph E. Enlow, *The Leader's Palette* (Bloomington, IN: Westbow, 2013), 3–11.

Leaders Are Stewards

Biblical leaders are entrusted with that which belongs to another. Paul had a keen sense of his responsibility for sharing the good news and for nurturing growth in grace among the churches of his day. As leader of his apostolic team, Paul wrote, "This is how one should regard us, as servants of Christ and stewards of the mysteries of God. Moreover, it is required of stewards that they be found faithful" (1 Cor 4:1–2). Paul instructed Titus that a church leader, "as God's steward, must be above reproach" (Titus 1:7).

In the first-century Roman world, a steward was a slave charged with management of his master's household. Indeed, the Greek word translated "steward" is a derivative of the word for house. Management of the homeowner's affairs was a solemn trust for which the steward was held accountable. Paul adopted this metaphor as a description of his calling and that of all church leaders. Both the gospel with which they are entrusted and "God's house" (i.e. the church) in which they serve belong to God. Diligence and integrity are indispensable qualities of a steward.

Leaders Are Servants

On the night of his arrest, Jesus reiterated to his disciples his most emphatic instruction on the leadership style which is to characterize his church: "And he said to them, 'The kings of the Gentiles exercise lordship over them, and those in authority over them are called benefactors. But not so with you. Rather, let the greatest among you become as the youngest, and the leader as one who serves. For who is the greater, one who reclines at table or one who serves? Is it not the one who reclines at table? But I am among you as the one who serves'" (Luke 22:25–27; cf. Matt 20:25–28).

Jesus notes two characteristics of the secular leadership so familiar in his day and ours. First, secular leaders "lord it over" their subjects. The word used is a common term implying the exercise of hierarchical supremacy, assuming priority of position or interest. We should note it is not necessary for hierarchical leadership to assume obnoxious proportions to fall under the judgment of Christ's "not so with you."

The second thing Jesus notes about secular leaders is that authoritarianism is valued. The ESV translates the expression "those in authority over them are called benefactors," but the NIV reads, "those who exercise authority over them call themselves Benefactors." Although the text legitimately can read either way, it is not necessary to quibble over our Lord's intent. Both readings provide an accurate picture of secular leadership. Authoritarian leaders routinely defend their dominance as beneficial to their subjects. Curiously, those subject to authoritarian leadership tend to attribute appropriateness to this pattern of leadership as well. Paulo Freire observed that the oppressed have a "fear of freedom" and find security in their oppression.[4]

In the face of this negative example, Jesus offered two positive principles for leadership in his church. First, Jesus addressed their concern for status: "the greatest among you [should] become as the youngest." The relational posture is one of humility. No one asserts rank. Instead of claiming supremacy, there is commitment "in humility [to] count others more significant than yourselves" (Phil 2:3).

The second principle Jesus stated called for a disposition toward service. "The leader [should be] as one who serves." If Jesus had not provided us with a model of servant leadership, perhaps these words would perplex us. Yet this is exactly the quality which best characterized his life and ministry. "I am among you," he could say, "as the one who serves." As those who train others for leadership in Christ's church, we do well to ask to what extent our colleagues and students affirm that this is an apt summary of our leadership as well.

Leaders Are Shepherds

Israel was an agrarian society in which the role of shepherd was familiar. The metaphor is significant not only for insight it provides into the appropriate responsibilities of church leaders, but especially for the light it throws on the way leaders relate to those whom they serve.

The writer of Hebrews refers to the Lord Jesus as "the great shepherd of the sheep" (Heb 13:20), and Peter employs the expression "the chief Shepherd" when speaking of Christ's second coming (1 Pet 5:4). In so doing, both of these passages point back to Jesus's Good Shepherd Discourse (John 10) as the beginning point for any study of Christian shepherding.

Several characteristics of the shepherd's relationship to the sheep form high points of Jesus's teaching in John 10. The shepherd knows the sheep

---

4. Paulo Freire, *Pedagogy of the Oppressed* (New York: Seabury, 1970), 31–32.

(v. 14), and he is known and trusted by them (vv. 3–5). He goes before them (v. 4), suggesting guidance, a modeling function, and concern for assuring their safety. Finally, the shepherd selflessly cares for the sheep, considering their safety and well-being, when necessary, above his own (v. 11). This self-description by Jesus of his ministry cannot help but challenge each of us who, at times, have been called "pastor."[5]

When Peter wrote to leaders of churches scattered along the southern shore of the Black Sea, he admonished them, "Be shepherds of God's flock that is under your care" (1 Pet 5:2 NIV). As he wrote these words, he must have recalled the same commission given to him by his Lord at a breakfast meeting beside another sea (John 21:16). It is interesting, therefore, to note the connotations this commission carried for Peter. Fortunately, he has spelled them out in his epistle.

The task of shepherding, Peter insists, should be undertaken "not under compulsion, but willingly" (1 Pet 5:2). In this contrast Peter has focused on both right and wrong attitudes which are evidenced, at times, in the ministries of all church leaders. As teachers and church leaders, we easily can find ourselves fulfilling our roles out of a sense of obligation rather than willingness. In doing so, Peter tells us, we have violated something of the essence of who the shepherd is.

Furthermore, the shepherd is "not pursuing dishonest gain, but eager to serve" (1 Pet 5:2 NIV). How often this is understood to affirm eagerness to serve the Lord! Yet that is not the force of the metaphor. A shepherd serves sheep! Sheep are self-willed, prone to wander, often smelly. The point of the text, however, is that the task of shepherding (which necessarily involves serving sheep) is undertaken eagerly. Not only is the shepherd characterized as possessing a willing attitude, he also has an eager heart.

Peter's third point of elaboration on the shepherding metaphor is so apt to the metaphor, but comes as a word of judgment upon much church leadership today. As shepherd, he reminds us, our proper relationship to the sheep is "not domineering over those in your charge, but being examples to the flock" (1 Pet 5:3). Because the sheep do not recognize the false shepherd (see John 10:5), the shepherd's tendency is to deal harshly with the sheep. It seems that

5. The English word "pastor" is derived from the Latin, in which it means "shepherd."

Bible translators have searched their vocabularies to find words harsh enough to express the connotations of Peter's description of the leadership style of the false shepherd. The ESV translates "not domineering over," the NIV employs "not lording it over," and the NEB resorts to "not tyrannizing over." Peter offers a sharp reminder to those who relate to the church in these ways: the sheep are not ours to treat as we will, but they have been entrusted to us. The pattern of appropriate leadership which Peter holds up, by contrast, is leadership by example. Here, again, we see the potency of the metaphor of the shepherd going before the sheep.

The metaphors of steward, servant, and shepherd commend a model of leadership that acknowledges a higher authority to whom the leader is accountable. The leader's role is to pursue the good of the community with sensitivity and care for all. In doing so, the leader humbly models the values to which the community aspires, providing an example for others to follow.

The Leader and Community Health

Leaders have a shaping effect on the culture of their communities. God's desire for our communities is *shalom* – life as he intends. In a *shalom* community people "learn to do good; seek justice, correct oppression; bring justice to the fatherless, [and] plead the widow's cause" (Isa 1:17; cf. Amos 5:24; Mic 6:8). Paul charged the leaders of the church in Ephesus to "Pay careful attention to yourselves and to all the flock, in which the Holy Spirit has made you overseers, to care for the church of God, which he obtained with his own blood" (Acts 20:28). Guarding, nurturing, and developing a community's culture is among a leader's highest responsibilities.

Closely related to the biblical pursuit of *shalom* is God's desire for oneness in the Christian community. Jesus prayed for oneness – unity, mutual care, single-mindedness – among his disciples (John 17:20–22) and said that love – mutual prioritizing of the other's good – should be the distinguishing quality of his church (John 13:35). Cultivating a culture of loving oneness, therefore, is a high priority for Christian leaders.

For this reason, one of the greatest challenges a leader can face is conflict in the Christian community. When conflict occurs, Western Christians are quick to turn to Matthew 18 which appears to prescribe a procedure of escalating confrontation for dealing with conflict.

> If your brother sins against you, go and tell him his fault, between you and him alone. If he listens to you, you have gained your brother. But if he does not listen, take one or two others along with you, that every charge may be established by the evidence of two or three witnesses. If he refuses to listen to them, tell it to the church. And if he refuses to listen even to the church, let him be to you as a Gentile and a tax collector. (Matt 18:15–17)

Thus, the first step toward dealing with conflict is personal confrontation with the offender. If he or she does not respond with apology and restitution, the second step is to repeat the confrontation in the presence of witnesses. Continued refusal to respond calls for public exposure and confrontation. If the offender is still unrepentant, the final step is exclusion of him or her from the community. In individualistic cultures which attach low value to personal honor and community acceptance, this procedure seems appropriate.

This approach is problematic, however, in communal cultures where community acceptance is a high value. Christians in those cultures struggle with the procedure outlined in Matthew 18. As a result, conflict among Christians often remains unresolved and the witness of churches in these cultures is compromised.

Leaders should not be surprised when conflict occurs among Christians. Although the redemption purchased by Christ is complete, we will enjoy that completeness only in heaven. Until then, the effects of Adam's fall continue to plague us. Conflict can result from simple misunderstandings, from incomplete information, from honest mistakes, or from differing responses to changing circumstances. It rarely is helpful to jump to the conclusion that conflict is sourced in ill-will or impure motives harbored by the offending party.

Elmer has pointed out that personal confrontation is not the only biblical model for dealing with conflict.[6] When David was offended by Nabal, God

---

6. Duane Elmer, *Cross-Cultural Conflict: Building Relationships for Effective Ministry* (Downers Grove, IL: InterVarsity, 1993). The following alternatives to personal confrontation are elaborated and illustrated by Elmer (65–133).

provided a mediator, Abigail, whom David credited with resolving the conflict and diverting his intention to overreact (1 Sam 25:1–35). Use of mediators to resolve conflict is common in communal cultures globally. Christians in any culture can find it liberating to recognize that God uses mediators, as well as direct confrontation, to resolve conflicts.

When Esther and her people were offended and threatened with extinction by Haman, Esther did not confront Haman. Rather, she appealed to a heathen king, acknowledging her vulnerability and requesting protection (Esth 7:1–7). There are times when God chooses to use those in authority to deliver his people, removing threats and resolving conflict. When faced with broken relationships, this alternative to direct confrontation may be especially appropriate if the offender is not a Christian brother or sister.

The conflict Nathan was called to address was between David and God (2 Sam 11:26 – 12:7). David had sinned, resulting in his broken relationship with God. God sent Nathan to confront David. Rather than charging David with his sin, Nathan told a story. David was enraged by Nathan's story and rendered his judgment, but soon recognized he had condemned himself. There are cultures where it is common to use story to resolve conflict, but this also can be an appropriate and effective method in any culture. A story that captures the essence of the offense can clarify issues without attacking the honor or prejudging the motives of the offender. A good story also exposes the contribution of each party to the relational brokenness.

David, as he fled from Absalom, was offended by Shimei. Rather than helping David, or even ignoring him, Shimei hurled curses at David as he fled Jerusalem (2 Sam 16:5–14). When Abishai offered to deal with Shimei's offense, however, David responded by accepting the offense and committing his defense to God.[7]

There are times, especially if other efforts have failed, when a Christian is wise simply to endure an offense and trust God as her or his protector and judge. So much conflict in the world and in the church would be avoided if individuals did not assume responsibility for pursuing every issue until they

---

7. Although David responded well in the moment, sadly he later took back responsibility for addressing Shimei's offense. On his death bed, he charged Solomon with Shimei's execution (1 Kgs 2:8–9).

receive the justice they believe they deserve. God knows the truth. Paul reminds his Roman readers and us that God owns the responsibility for justice; we do not (Rom 12:19–21).

As leaders promote *shalom* and resolve conflict within the community, they have a shaping impact on the culture of that community. The culture of the community, in turn, shapes the lives of members of the community, individually and collectively. This culture-shaping is an important aspect of leadership.

Leadership and Power

If interpersonal conflict is among the greatest challenges faced by the leader, abuse of power is among the greatest temptations the leader faces. Power is the capacity to effect change. Nothing affects relationships in a community more directly, both for good and for ill, than the way power is exercised. As Christians, our primary obligation is to understand and reflect God's attitude toward and use of power as revealed in the Bible.

Power, inherently, is neither good nor bad; God is all-powerful. Fallen humans, however, find power enticing and addictive. Furthermore, they are prone to employ power selfishly and (not infrequently) abusively.[8] There is no need to renounce power but it must be stewarded.

Jesus rebuffed Satan's temptations to employ power for his own benefit (Matt 4:3–4), to amass political power (Matt 4:5–7),[9] and to acquire the absolute power of ownership (Matt 4:8–9). Rather than establishing himself in Jerusalem, the political and religious center of the Jewish nation, Jesus chose to live in Capernaum, a remote fishing village (Matt 4:13). The primary focus of his ministry was Galilee (Mark 1:38–39, known colloquially as "Galilee of the Gentiles." Rather than urging those whose lives he touched to spread his

---

8. For a development of this theme, see Andy Crouch, *Playing God: Redeeming the Gift of Power* (Downers Grove, IL: InterVarsity, 2013).

9. Below the pinnacle was the temple square. First-century Jews were well aware of Scriptures promising a coming Messiah who would establish an eternal kingdom centered in Jerusalem. What could have been more welcome than to see one descend into the temple square, apparently from heaven, as Elijah had been taken up? If Jesus had descended, as Satan suggested, he would have been recognized immediately as the promised Messiah. His popularity would have been instantaneous and his political power unrivaled.

fame, he repeatedly asked them to tell no one.[10] This baffled even his brothers (John 7:1–9). When his disciples quarreled over who was greatest – which among them exercised the most power and authority – he condemned their aspirations to greatness and charged them to emulate his example of humility and servanthood (Luke 22:25–27; cf. Matt 20:25–28).

God is all-powerful but he has not reserved all power to himself. In creating humans in his image, he has empowered us, as well. God is creator of all that exists, yet he invites us to share in his creative activity as we reproduce and populate the world he created. He created all plants and animals but invites us to tend the earth and steward its bounty. God has revealed truth about himself, about ourselves, and about how we are to live but he commits to us teaching our children and ordering our society. God cares for the needy but he invites us to participate in their care. God has provided redemption sufficient for all people but he commits to us the task of carrying this good news to the world. God not only invites us to participate in his work, he also empowers us to do the work he gives to us.

Scripture consistently portrays God's use of power in two primary ways: God shares his power with his creatures, and he uses his power to serve. Jesus came to reveal God's character and God's desire for relationship with his creatures (John 1:18). We can understand God's use of power by observing Jesus. Jesus faced life as we do (Heb 2:17) and demonstrated the divine power available to us through prayer, faith, and the Holy Spirit.[11] Jesus exercised this power to heal the sick, to cast out demons, to feed the hungry, and to raise the dead. Jesus consistently used his power to serve others. When threatened, in the garden of Gethsemane, he declined to summon spiritual powers to save himself (Matt 26:53–54); instead he gave himself for us.

---

10. See Matt 9:30; 12:15–16; Mark 1:42–44; 5:43; 7:36; 8:26. Jesus's choice to use power to serve and to empower others, rather than to serve himself, resolves this mystery, known by scholars as "the Messianic secret."

11. When asked to explain his miracles, Jesus never referenced his divine omnipotence. Rather, when asked by the disciples why they could not cast an evil spirit from an epileptic boy, Jesus said it was because the only effective resource is prayer (Mark 9:28–29). When the disciples marveled at Jesus's stilling of a storm at sea, Jesus attributed their inability to lack of faith (Luke 8:22–25). When pressed on his source of power to cast out demons, Jesus attributed his work to "the finger of God," i.e. the power of the Holy Spirit (Luke 11:19–20).

Jesus also distributed his power to others. After preaching the kingdom of God, he sent others to do the same and empowered them for this ministry (Luke 9:1–2; 10:1, 17). After rising from death, Jesus sent and empowered the disciples to continue his ministry (John 20:21–23). Jesus also promised empowerment for global evangelism (Luke 24:49; Acts 1:8), a promise dramatically fulfilled on the day of Pentecost (Acts 2:1–41).

As teachers and models for our students, God calls us to follow the example of our Lord. We must steward the power we hold, taking the role of servant, and using our capacities to serve and to empower others.

The Spiritual Life of the Leader

Life transformation is God's work. He graciously calls us as his servants and uses us as his instruments but we cannot do God's work in our own strength. Ministry effectiveness flows out of familiarity with God's Word and personal intimacy with God. If the graduates of our seminaries are to bring transformational change to the churches and communities in which they minister, they must be men and women who know God intimately.

Spiritual intimacy does not occur naturally. The world, the flesh, and the devil oppose growth in grace, in holiness, and in ministry effectiveness. Spiritual intimacy must be cultivated; it requires time and intentional commitment. If the ministries of our graduates are to bring the transforming power of the gospel into the lives of those in their communities, we must provide an environment that cultivates spiritual discipline.

We cannot lead where we have not gone. Unless we are men and women who know God intimately and who practice the disciplines we intend to cultivate in our students, our efforts will be unsuccessful. The Luke 6:40 Principle, mentioned above, is painfully evident in too many of our schools. Faculty members who allow pursuit of scholarly disciplines, inflation of their ministry status, or other concerns to encroach on their own spiritual life graduate students whose spiritual lives are shallow and whose ministries lack divine power. To fulfill our calling to equip others for ministry, we first must cultivate our own inner life with Christ.

It is most reassuring to know that this is God's intention for us. If we consider why God created this universe, the only conceivable reason is that he chose to create. He certainly did not need to create; he is and forever has been completely free of need of anything outside of himself. As Trinity, even relational fulfillment is satisfied in the love and communication eternally shared by Father, Son, and Holy Spirit. At some point in eternity past, however, God chose to expand that eternal circle of relationship by creating others like himself, other persons whom he could love, with whom he could communicate, and who freely could love and communicate with him in return. It is specifically to fulfill this desire that you and I and every person on this planet exist.

God desires an intimate, personal relationship with you and with each of your students. He desires you to provide a model of spiritual maturity and intimacy that your students can emulate. He also desires that the community of our campuses and of his church would reflect the relational unity of the Trinity.

Evangelical Christians understand the necessity of the Scriptures for spiritual health, typically engaging Scripture in different ways. "Rapid reading" offers an overview; it develops familiarity with the broad sweep of Scripture. We may read an entire book at one sitting or adopt a plan to read through the Bible in a year. "Analytical reading" seeks to discern the meaning of a limited passage. This is serious Bible study; it employs the methods of biblical introduction (study of the authorship, historical context, occasion, and date of a passage, and of its place within the progress of revelation) and exegesis (grammatical study of a passage and word studies, taken in light of the immediate and larger contexts). "Thematic reading" intends to grasp the teaching of Scripture on a selected topic or theme and to see it in relationship to other biblical revelation. This is theological study; it follows a topic or theme in the writings of a given author or genre (often referred to as biblical theology) or across the scope of biblical revelation (the approach of systematic theology).

These approaches to Bible reading typically are emphasized in evangelical seminaries. This is appropriate, since an accurate and faithful understanding of the Word is critical for all ministry leaders in order to avoid error and to teach truth. Note, however, that "rapid reading," "analytical reading," and "thematic reading" focus on acquiring information and developing understanding. God desires us to understand his revealed truth accurately but he intends that understanding to be instrumental – it should lead to obedience, conformity to his character (i.e. Christlikeness), which, in turn, should lead to intimacy with God.

A fourth method of reading the Bible is "attentive reading." In attentive reading, the sole purpose is to meet with God, to hear his voice as he speaks to me today. We approach the Scriptures as the principal medium through which God reveals himself, through which he relates to us individually, and through which he speaks into our lives.

Attentive reading is the primary activity of the Christian mystics. When attentive reading is not informed by broader and deeper understandings of God's Word, it can lead to unbiblical error. Fear of such abuse has led evangelical Christians to shun, or even discourage, attentive reading. Too often, in the process, we have settled for a correct understanding of God's truth at the expense of the intimacy with God that our souls crave and that God himself desires. In recent years, however, some evangelicals have rediscovered the value of attentive reading of Scripture.[12]

Attentive reading cannot be mandated but it can be modeled and discussed. The importance of intimacy with Christ in the life of the Christian should be emphasized throughout our curricula and the life of our schools. Faculty members should speak openly and often of the importance of attentive reading in their own walk with Christ. The school's administration should insure that helpful literature on Christian spirituality is included in the library and the faculty should make a point of recommending to students books that foster spiritual development.

Faculty members also may offer to mentor students in the discipline of attentive reading and in formation of the spiritual life.[13] To do so effectively, however, demands time; it is unlikely to happen if faculty members are

---

12. Christian classics, ancient and modern, include Augustine, Bernard of Clairvaux, Thomas à Kempis, John Bunyan, Andrew Murray, A. W. Tozer, and Dietrich Bonhoeffer. Faculty members and students may also find the following works helpful: Richard Foster, *Celebration of Discipline: The Path to Spiritual Growth*, 3rd ed. (New York: HarperCollins, 1998); Eugene Peterson, *Eat This Book: A Conversation in the Art of Spiritual Reading* (Grand Rapids: Eerdmans, 2006); Dallas Willard, Trilogy: *Hearing God: Developing a Conversational Relationship with God* (2012); *The Spirit of the Disciplines: Understanding How God Changes Lives* (1999); and *The Divine Conspiracy: Rediscovering Our Hidden Life in God* (1998; all Downers Grove, IL: InterVarsity); M. Robert Mulholland, Jr., *Invitation to a Journey: A Road Map for Spiritual Formation* (Downers Grove: InterVarsity, 1993); and Brian K. Rice, *The Exercises, Volume One: Conversations* (York, PA: Leadership ConneXtions International, 2012).

13. For guidance on spiritual mentoring, see Keith R. Anderson and Randy D. Reese, *Spiritual Mentoring: A Guide for Seeking and Giving Direction* (Downers Grove, IL: InterVarsity, 1999).

overloaded with courses and administrative responsibilities. An alternative may be for the school to recruit pastors and alumni from the area who agree to assist in the preparation of a new generation of ministers by spiritually mentoring students. If the school requests help in this way, it also should provide training and recognition for those who serve as spiritual mentors.

Explicit Curricula, Implicit Curricula, and Curricular Dissonance

In the following chapters, we will discuss a process for developing curricula for transformational education. It is important to recognize, however, that every school has more than one curriculum and some schools have many. The published curriculum – the list of courses, studies, and lectureships offered, plus experiences required – constitutes the "explicit curriculum" of the school. It is stated, affirmed, and required; deviations from the explicit curriculum must be formally approved by the school's academic leadership.

Parallel to the explicit curriculum is the "implicit curriculum."[14] The implicit curriculum is comprised of the many factors that shape the life and learning of the student in addition to the explicit curriculum. These include the ethos of the school, the culture of the campus or learning community, and the values modeled by members of the faculty, the school's administrators, and staff.

When the explicit curriculum and implicit curriculum are aligned, the educational effect is maximized. Any divergence between the explicit curriculum and the implicit curriculum, however, creates dissonance that erodes the effectiveness of the explicit curriculum and the stated mission of the school.

An educational truism states that the implicit curriculum always overpowers the explicit curriculum. Irrespective of lessons taught in the classroom, students will follow the example of their teachers rather than

---

14. The implicit curriculum often is referred to as "the hidden curriculum," a construct initially proposed by Philip Jackson (*Life in Classrooms* [New York: Holt, Rinehart and Winston, 1968]). That term is unfortunate, however, since it may suggest that this curriculum is promoted surreptitiously or with devious intent. That never was the intended meaning and the simple contrast between explicit and implicit serves much better.

their words. This sobering reality underlines the urgency of whole-campus commitment to education for transformation of life and ministry. In a school's offices, classrooms, and kitchen, leadership matters.

To a profound degree, the primary curricula of our schools are not those we publish; the faculty is the curriculum. It is the way we handle God's Word. It is the way we relate to one another, to students, and to others on and off campus. It is the way we relate to Christ's church. It is the way we relate to the non-Christian world around us. That is the most important and most effective curriculum of our schools. The explicit curriculum is important primarily as a medium through which we communicate to students who we are and to what we are committed. The faculty *is* the curriculum!

6

The Role of Stakeholders in Curriculum Development

For ministry education to be truly transformative, it is not enough for individual teachers to employ interactive and dialogical teaching methods or to model the truths they teach. Pursuit of ministry education that transforms must be a commitment of an entire faculty and must be engaged intentionally, purposefully, wholeheartedly.

Traditional approaches to curriculum development – those that place ownership with the faculty and are modeled on curricula of peer institutions – cannot generate transformative ministry education. The scholarship of a faculty is valuable, an asset to be stewarded for the benefit of the church, but scholastic passions of the academy typically differ from the foci of church and community ministries. Curricula developed exclusively by scholars produce scholars, even when their intentions are otherwise. It is no accident that many students enter seminary with a passion for ministry and graduate with a passion for scholarship and a career in teaching.

To change this unintended effect of our seminary programs, curriculum development must be undertaken in collaboration with the church. It is the seminary's stakeholders – its constituent churches and ministries – that are intimately engaged in and aware of those ministries for which students must be prepared. The members of the seminary's governing board have legal responsibility for defining the mission and values of the school. Traditionally, however, the board's role in determining curricula – the most direct means by which that mission is pursued and those values are conveyed – has been negligible.

To invite the seminary's stakeholders, its board, and its administrators to collaborate in developing the curriculum of the seminary is to surrender a prerogative faculty members traditionally have guarded and prized. Collaborative curriculum development entails surrendering the power to determine what we will teach. As we have seen, power is addictive. Surrender of power is always resisted, yet this is the path of servanthood. If seminaries are to serve the church, as our mission statements typically profess, we must choose the path of collaborative development of the curricula we will teach.

This is not to suggest that the faculty has no role in curriculum development. Collaboration is different from disengagement or abdication. Indeed, the faculty has a critical role that stakeholders and boards are ill-equipped to perform. The faculty remains intimately engaged but the task is shared and roles are redefined. This chapter and the next offer an approach to developing curricula that can orient the seminary toward the church and that can create an environment in which transformative ministry education becomes a reality.[1]

Clarifying the Mission of the Seminary

The beginning point in transformative educational planning is clarification of the mission of the seminary. In that task the seminary's governing board is the primary actor. Most Bible schools and seminaries have a mission statement but too often the statement has been developed as a marketing instrument rather than as a clear, concise, and cogent statement of the seminary's purpose.

Rather than a marketing tool, it is helpful to think of the mission statement as a calling of God to be stewarded by the seminary community. The task should be approached with full information but also in earnest prayer. If our purpose is to be and to model a divinely guided community in pursuit of God's calling, then prayer is the essential context for any discussion of God's calling and our mission.

A fruitful approach to determining the mission of the seminary is to look at the constituencies the seminary intends to serve. Are these congregations, their

---

1. An early and less-developed version of the approach to curriculum development described in this and the following chapter appeared in Robert W. Ferris, ed., *Establishing Ministry Training: A Manual for Programme Developers* (Pasadena, CA: William Carey Library, 1995), 23–49.

denominational or associational structures, as well as the church's ministry and missional agencies, well led? Many ministry training institutions seek to serve a broader evangelical community of churches and parachurch ministries. In such cases, it is helpful to focus on a few specific churches and ministries with which the seminary is more closely related lest important recognitions are missed in a plethora of diverse messages.

Another factor in determining the mission of the seminary is to observe recent graduates of the school. Where are they serving? How are they doing? What do they perceive to be areas in which their training served them well and those in which they wish they had been better served? If the school's mission statement does not describe the ministry of most graduates or if many graduates report significant gaps in their learning, either the mission statement should be adjusted or the school's curriculum should be aligned with the school's mission.

Around the world today, many churches function with inadequately trained leadership. It is not necessary to embrace or endorse a clerical paradigm to recognize that leadership's unfamiliarity with Scripture places a church in jeopardy of error and confusion. If the board's survey of its constituent church and supporting ministries reveals numerous untrained or under-trained leaders, addressing this lack may be the single most important mission to which the seminary is called.

The seminary's board, rather than the faculty, is entrusted with this task of determining the needs of the school's constituencies. A good governing board is comprised of men and women who are leaders in church, business, the professions, and the community. They often are more closely related to the seminary's constituent communities than full-time members of the faculty and may be less swayed by academic allegiances than are faculty members. The board deserves the full support of the faculty as it undertakes the task of defining the seminary's mission.

Recruiting a Stakeholders' Panel

Clarity of mission is important. The next step, however, is to identify the characteristics of a graduate who is equipped to minister as the mission statement envisions. The seminary's stakeholders – its constituent churches, parachurch ministries, and alumni[2] – are the right ones to develop the profile of an ideal graduate. Since it is not practical for all stakeholders to be involved, a representative panel of stakeholders is needed. These should be men and women who are model practitioners, deeply engaged in the ministries of the seminary's constituent churches. These model practitioners will exhibit the qualities and skills required to function effectively as described in the seminary's mission.

Given the critical role of the Stakeholders' Panel, those recruited to serve on the panel must be selected carefully. The school's administration is best positioned to handle this task. In consultation with the seminary's constituent churches and ministries, with alumni, and with the faculty, the school's president, principal, or rector should identify and recruit individuals to serve on the Stakeholders' Panel. If the mission of the school is well focused, the panel need not be large; six to eight model stakeholders is sufficient.[3] Care should be taken to avoid appointing more than ten to the Stakeholders' Panel, since this typically complicates, rather than expedites, the work of the panel.

Developing a Ministry Leadership Profile

Once the Stakeholders' Panel has been recruited, it is necessary to set a date for the panel to do its work, to identify a facilitator for the profiling task, and to prepare a meeting space for the panel. Members of the Stakeholders' Panel should be requested to allocate a full day for the work of the panel. It is advantageous, if possible, to begin one evening and to continue through the following day. Although members of the panel may resist allocating that much time, it is not wise to shorten the time needed to generate a profile of

---

2. "Stakeholders" are all those who hold a stake in – i.e. who are affected either beneficially or adversely by – the seminary and its graduates. In addition to the groups mentioned, students and faculty members are stakeholders. They should not, however, be represented on the Stakeholders' Panel. Students' interests are best represented by the mature perspectives of alumni and the seminary's constituent churches. The contribution of faculty members to developing the seminary's curriculum is significant but comes at a later point in the process. Premature engagement by the faculty can skew curriculum development in unproductive ways.

3. If the mission of the seminary is complex, requiring more than one program, it is best to focus on one program at a time, beginning with the program that addresses the most urgent need among the seminary's constituencies. Hopefully, this also will be the seminary's largest program.

an ideal seminary graduate. This task is critically important to the ministry of the seminary; it deserves the priority it demands.

The facilitator chosen to lead the profiling task can enhance or diminish the usefulness of the profile produced. A staff member of a nonformal education program in the seminary's region may be able to serve the school best.[4] Alternatively, a member of the school's practical theology faculty – a Christian education, pastoral theology, or missiology teacher – may be the best local choice to facilitate the profiling exercise. The task of the facilitator is to manage and guide the process without influencing the shape of the resulting profile. A school's president and faculty members who teach in other areas typically find this difficult.

A classroom or meeting room can serve well for the profiling task. Stakeholders may be seated at a large table or in chairs arranged in a semicircle. The task will be pursued collectively, so it is important for members of the Stakeholders' Panel to have eye contact with one another. An easel with newsprint, a large whiteboard or blackboard, and a generous supply of Post-it notes may be needed. A computer and digital projector also may be helpful. A staff assistant is needed to support the profiling exercise and to create a record of the work of the Stakeholders' Panel.

When the Stakeholders' Panel has been convened, the work of developing a ministry leadership profile can begin. The profile describes the characteristics – essential abilities and character – of the seminary's "ideal graduate." An ideal graduate is a student who has completed his or her course of studies and who, therefore, is fully prepared to serve the church and community as envisioned in the seminary's mission statement. Since each seminary has a unique calling from God and serves a unique constituency, the characteristics of an ideal graduate, while similar to those of other seminaries in basic ways, also will be unique to each school. Adopting another school's graduate profile is never advisable. In addition to the uniqueness of each school's mission, the profiling exercise is beneficial in bringing practical clarity to the curricular mandate of the faculty.

---

4. GATE Associates are trained to facilitate profiling exercises.

Set a Context for Generating a Ministry Leadership Profile

The facilitator should create a sense of anticipation about the profiling process. It is important for participants to know why they are involved in the exercise and what outcome is expected. Questions and discussion should be encouraged so that all participants understand what they are expected to contribute to the profiling task. It also may be necessary to clarify schedules and other administrative details.

It is unfortunate, but true, that we naturally focus on formal (academic) and pragmatic (skill) factors when identifying qualifications for any role. A useful technique for establishing biblical perspective regarding ministry qualifications is to ask participants to review 1 Timothy 3:1–7, 2 Timothy 2:24–25, and Titus 1:6–9, three passages which describe the qualifications of a church leader. Using a whiteboard, make three parallel columns and label them "Knowledge," "Skills," and "Character." Figure 6.1 illustrates how the columns may look.

Knowledge	Skills	Character

Figure 6.1: Sample Chart for Qualifications of a Church Leader

Taking the listed passages one at a time, invite members of the panel, in succession, to read a verse or two and to identify the heading under which each qualification should be listed. (There is duplication among these lists, but it is not necessary to reflect the duplication on the chart.)

This exercise usually takes only about fifteen minutes but it may precipitate a longer discussion. Participants quickly will recognize that most New Testament qualifications describe the character of the church leader and therefore fall into the third column. "Knowledge" is almost unmentioned in these passages. If participants have not seen this before, it will challenge their assumptions about priorities in ministry training.

A common question relates to the scant notice given to "knowledge" qualifications. It would be easy (but dangerous!) to conclude that knowledge is unimportant in spiritual leadership. A more insightful perspective recognizes that knowledge is given by God, not as an end in itself (that is when "knowledge puffs up") but as a means toward holiness and ministry. Knowledge is important because of the way God uses it to shape our lives and the way he enables us to use it in the lives of others. Thus, God develops the many listed character qualities in us when we fill our minds and hearts with his Word and when we obey it. This helps us understand the Bible's emphasis on "obeying" or "doing" the truth.

Other knowledge is essential to effective skills in ministry. Every skill assumes or requires certain knowledge. A medical doctor must know a great deal about the human body, diseases, and medicines in order to know how to treat patients. A launderer must know about the characteristics of fabrics, dyes, and stains in order to know how to remove a spot without destroying a garment. Likewise, a Christian must know God's Word before she or he can know how to obey it or teach others to do so.

Knowledge typically is valued for one of two reasons. Sometimes knowledge is valued because it affords prestige or power. Elitism and demagoguery are inconsistent, however, with Christian virtues.

Knowledge also may be valued for its usefulness. It enables us to be or to do what otherwise is impossible – note the illustrations of the medical doctor and the launderer above. Thus, knowledge has instrumental value. This is not to disparage a lively curiosity but merely to acknowledge that satisfying curiosities is not the purpose of ministry training programs. Our purpose is to equip ministry leaders who, in turn, are able to equip others.

Recognizing the instrumental value of knowledge – nourishing holiness and enabling ministry – helps us understand the importance of "knowledge" qualifications for ministry. Understanding that the role and value of knowledge is instrumental, however, also clarifies why curriculum development must be undertaken collaboratively, engaging both the seminary faculty and its stakeholders. Stakeholders – specifically, the model practitioners recruited to the Stakeholders' Panel – are best able to identify the skills and character qualities required for effectiveness in ministry. The seminary faculty, on the other hand, is best equipped to identify knowledge needed for effective exercise of the skills identified and which the Holy Spirit typically uses to cultivate the identified character qualities.

If the schedule for the profiling exercise begins with an evening session, as suggested, it is appropriate and helpful to invite the seminary faculty to join the Stakeholders' Panel for this examination of the biblical qualities of a church leader and for clarification of the respective roles of the Stakeholders' Panel and the seminary faculty. Without protracting the evening, it can be encouraging and wholesome to invite members of the faculty to pray for the members of the Stakeholders' Panel as they undertake their work the following day.

Identify General Areas of Qualification

The initial task of the Stakeholders' Panel is to identify the skill competencies and character qualities required for effectiveness in the ministry leadership role described in the seminary's mission statement. This is best approached as a two-step process.

First, general skill areas and character areas are identified, then each of these general areas is analyzed to identify specific competencies or qualities that demonstrate or reflect the characteristic identified. Note that the difference between the two steps relates to level of analysis, rather than kind of activity. It is important, at this point, that participants understand their task and discipline themselves to think in broad categories.

The most efficient way to identify skill and character areas essential to effectiveness in ministry is for members of the Stakeholders' Panel to reflect on the things they do and the ways they are challenged daily, monthly, and even occasionally. The context should be a "green light" or "brainstorming" session in which examples are mentioned without comment or questions. As activities (reflecting skill areas) and challenges (testing character areas) are mentioned, the assistant should record them on Post-it notes or on a whiteboard while the facilitator elicits additional responses.

It is important to bear in mind that the participants' experience in ministry is the primary resource and focus of the "green light" session. The task is not to exegete the biblical qualifications or to discuss implications of examples offered. This activity draws on the experience of participants to identify qualification areas. A question like one of the following may help participants begin identifying qualification areas:

- What qualities and skills enable you to be an effective ministry leader?
- What qualities and skills distinguish your most effective ministries?

When the "green light" session begins to slow, the list generated should be reviewed to insure that insights derived from the study of biblical qualifications are included.

The next step is to consolidate the list into general areas of skills and character. If the assistant has recorded each item mentioned in the "green light" session on a separate Post-it note, these can be posted randomly to a wall or whiteboard to be observed by the group. Then, working as a group, participants should cluster individual items to identify distinct skill or character areas. A useful list will include six to ten skill areas and a similar number of character areas. If a larger number of areas is identified, the facilitator should encourage participants to explore broader categories which consolidate these lists even more without losing important skills or character factors mentioned in the "green light" session.

The result will be a minimal list of clearly identified areas for which future ministry leaders must be trained. It is important that all participants have an opportunity to review the list and to express concurrence that the areas they consider important have been included. To proceed in the profiling process is not wise if even a few participants are dissatisfied with the list of qualification areas. It is best to solicit vocal statements of support from all members of the Stakeholders' Panel. If the facilitator has been attentive to comments and concerns expressed during the process of consolidation, these endorsements will usually be quickly expressed.

Identify Specific Skill Competencies and Character Qualities

The focus now shifts to analyzing specific competencies and qualities that evidence each of the twelve to twenty areas identified. Skill competencies and character qualities should be expressed as statements of observable behavior. Ultimately, these will be arranged in a profile chart (Figure 6.2) with the general area to the left and specific competencies or qualities arrayed to the right.

Quality or Skill Area	Specific Qualities or Competencies		
Interpersonal relations	Applies biblical principles to relationships	Listens to others and responds appropriately	Manages interpersonal conflict well

Figure 6.2: Sample Profile Chart

Although the order in which the qualification areas are considered is unimportant, it is wise to begin with a skill area which seems simple and straightforward. Encourage each member of the Stakeholders' Panel to think of specific competencies needed in the skill area selected. As when identifying skill and character areas, it is best to employ a "green light" procedure first, then to consolidate suggested items to arrive at a manageable list of competencies or qualities to be included in the profile of an ideal graduate.

It is not unusual for the "green light" activity to generate twenty or twenty-five suggestions for a single skill or character area. These, then, should be clustered and reframed as four to eight specific skill competencies or character qualities. Each item should be expressed in a succinct statement of observable behavior expressed with an action verb.

As you consider each proposed skill competency or character quality, you will want to ask, "Is this observable? If so, how?" Asking these questions will help the Stakeholders' Panel sharpen each item in such a way that it will be useful in the eventual design of a curriculum which recognizes or develops the competency or quality.

It is important to note that most character qualities will be difficult to articulate in directly observable terms, but specific behaviors which indicate a presence of these traits may be more easily identified. For example, the item "Christlikeness" is difficult to observe but behaviors reflecting Christlikeness, such as "Is considerate of others" or "Serves others readily," are more specific and observable. A skillful facilitator will help the panel come up with the right verb and phrasing for each item.

The product of this exercise should be a list of succinct statements under each general skill and character area which expresses observable evidence of readiness to provide the type of ministry leadership identified in the seminary's mission statement. Each area may have four to eight succinct skill competency or character quality statements. If there are many more, it is likely the area is too broad and, under analysis, a natural subdivision will be apparent.

Once the specific skill competencies and character qualities for all areas have been identified and listed, they should be reviewed by the panel to assure appropriate completeness. A competency or quality may be removed from an area if duplication is observed or it may be reworded to express more clearly the underlying observation or concern.

Figure 6.3 is a profile of an ideal Indian missionary. We have chosen to provide this example because it is a profile quite different from that of most seminary graduates, yet it is an example of a profile chart. The task of the Stakeholders' Panel is to develop a similar chart that describes the ideal graduate of your seminary.

Skill Areas	Competencies				
Communicates Effectively	Conversation fluency	Good public speaker	Writes clearly and effectively	Keeps a journal	
Builds Relationships	Understands personalities	Accepts others	Listens attentively	Manages conflict	Delegates responsibility
Communicates Cross-Culturally	Exposes ethnocentrism	Adopts local culture	Learns local language	Learns nonverbals	Identifies with people
Learns a Language	Recognizes importance	Builds friendships	Learns new sounds	Imitates local speech	Patiently perseveres
Evangelizes and Preaches	Expresses Christian love	Discerns readiness	Exposes errors	Applies the Bible	Alternative methods
Teaches and Disciples	Leads a group Bible study	Makes truth simple	Communicates clearly	A servant-leader	
Plants the Church	Surveys the field	Sets goals and targets	Evangelizes appropriately	Trains new believers	Trains in evangelism

Character Areas	Qualities				
Spiritually Mature	Spiritually discerning	Reflects fruit of the Spirit	Increasingly Christlike	Loves reading the Bible	Committed to a local church
Zeal for Evangelism	Burdened for the unreached	Committed to pray	Gives to missions	Joyful in suffering	Embraces a simple lifestyle
Disciplined and Accountable	Steward of time and money	Controls own speech	Trustworthy	Mutually submissive	Exercises right authority
Adaptable	Willing to adapt	A humble learner	Positive and hopeful	Patient	Values other cultures
Rightly Related to God	Submissive to God	Prayerfully adores God	Knows God's sovereignty	Trusts God's faithfulness	
Rightly Related to Family	Guards quality family time	Leads family spiritually	Models openness and love	Encourages family	
Rightly Related to Community	Respected by neighbors	Appreciates others	Helpful	Empathetic	

Figure 6.3: Qualifications for Indian Missionaries[5]

Endorse the Profile Chart

When the Stakeholders' Panel has completed identification of skill and character areas requisite for functioning effectively as stated in the seminary's mission statement, members of the panel can take a break while the facilitator and assistant construct the profile chart. This is done by creating two tables, one for required skills and a second for required character traits. In each table, skill areas and character areas are listed in the first column, one per row. The competencies or qualities needed effectively to employ that skill or to manifest

---

5. This sample profile is an abbreviated summary of work done by participants in a workshop sponsored by the Indian Missions Association held 21–23 September 1992 in Chennai (then Madras), Tamil Nadu, India. The original document appears as appendix C in Ferris, *Establishing Ministry Training*.

that quality then are arrayed to the right of each skill or character area, as illustrated in Figure 6.3.

When the profile chart is ready for review, members of the Stakeholders' Panel should be given opportunity to make final adjustments prior to endorsement. Any modifications called for should be made to the satisfaction of the whole panel. Again, it is important to call for verbal or symbolic (e.g. standing or signing) endorsement of the profile chart by each member of the panel.

When the profile chart has been endorsed, the primary task of the panel is complete. In recognition of their contribution, it is appropriate to provide each member of the panel with a copy of the profile they created of an effective ministry leader. Before concluding the session, the panel should be advised that their service will be requested again to review and assess a curriculum prepared by the faculty that is designed to address the training goals represented by the profile they created.

7

The Role of the Faculty in Curriculum Development

A profile chart provides a visual picture of the training task but it is not a curriculum of studies.[1] Developing a curriculum that equips the seminary's entering students to function in ministry as envisioned in the profile of an effective ministry leader is the responsibility of the seminary's faculty. This is a demanding responsibility which will require full participation and substantial collaboration among all faculty members, guided by the Holy Spirit. A thorough understanding of the theory and methods of transformational education, discussed above, will be invaluable in fulfilling this responsibility.

As we have seen, the profile of an ideal graduate identifies the skill competencies and character qualities needed for effective ministry leadership in the context of the school's primary constituency. At that point we recognized the importance of knowledge but noted that the value of knowledge lies in its instrumental effect. We asked model practitioners to defer the question of what students need to know and to focus on identifying what they must be and must be able to do. Now it becomes the responsibility of the faculty to

---

1. Educational terms are used differently according to the traditions of each culture. In some contexts, what we have termed a "curriculum of studies" or "curriculum" is referred to as a "course," and what we term a "course" is referred to as a "subject." As we use these terms, a "curriculum" refers to all the requirements for a certificate, diploma, or degree offered by a school, or, in non-formal settings, to the complete plan for a workshop or seminar. If a school awards more than one diploma or degree, each will have its own curriculum. Each curriculum consists of "courses" which address the specific character qualities, skills, and supporting knowledge the curriculum is designed to develop. Each unit within a course, typically one to three hours in length, we term a "lesson" and for each lesson we develop a "lesson plan." Thus, a "course" typically consists of several "lessons," and a "curriculum" is comprised of several "courses."

employ the profile of an ideal graduate to develop a curriculum of studies that will equip graduating students for effectiveness in ministry.

Accept the Profile Prepared by the Stakeholders' Panel

It is important for the faculty to resist the strong temptation to debate the appropriateness and comprehensiveness of competencies and qualities included in the profile. When faculty members debate the skill and character areas included in the profile, they devalue the work of the Stakeholders' Panel. The purpose of the panel was to gain a fresh perspective on the mission of the seminary, one shaped by practitioners who daily experience the realities of ministry and who model the skills and character the seminary must develop. Debate easily becomes a means of advancing our own disciplinary interests, polarizing the faculty. It is vital for faculty members to assume that *practitioners* know best what skill competencies and character qualities are needed and that *faculty members* know best how to train toward those outcomes. The integrity of the curriculum development task depends on respecting the role and responsibility of each group.

Although, as a faculty, you accept the profile created by the Stakeholders' Panel, it may not be necessary to teach all of the skills or to develop all of the character qualities identified in the profile. Your typical student already may have some of the desired skills and character qualities when arriving on campus. This is not a problem. Indeed, the more incoming students reflect the characteristics of your ideal graduate, the greater your capacity to develop in them the capacities and qualities needed for effectiveness in ministry. It is likely, however, that your typical incoming student will have only a few of these skill competencies and character qualities. Those qualities that are common among incoming students can be listed as entrance requirements for your seminary program. When a competency or quality is specified as an entrance requirement, you no longer need to develop it. You can cross it off the list of qualities you must develop. The remaining skill competencies and character qualities are your "Program Goals."

Identify Knowledge and Experience Required for Skill Competencies

Skills are gained through instruction and practice. Typically, effective use of skills also requires knowledge that supports or is required to use the skill. It is informative to understand alternative approaches to personal evangelism and to gain practice in sharing the gospel under the guidance of a mentor but it also is necessary to acquire knowledge that supports evangelistic engagement. Effective evangelists are familiar with biblical passages on repentance, faith, and forgiveness, as well as with apologetic responses to issues commonly raised in their context. Similarly, other competencies require supporting knowledge. Without such knowledge, effectiveness in ministry is impossible.

When identifying knowledge needed to support the listed competencies, it may be useful to distinguish between "information" and "principles," since these are taught using different methods. We need to recall "information" (or recall how to access it) but "principles" (or "theory" – the underlying structure that reveals the relationship of multiple facts) must be elaborated with supporting evidence and rationale.

The faculty should engage one skill area at a time. As the faculty addresses each competency listed for that skill, it should ask, "What must the student know in order to do this?" In this question, the most important word is "must." As soon as the issue of "knowledge goals" is opened, generations of intellectual traditions rush upon us, quickly suggesting long lists of "important" knowledge, often closely paralleling existing curricula.

The issue of traditional curricula is complex. Curriculum developers can never afford to disregard information simply because it is part of a traditional curriculum. It is dangerous, however, to discount the extent to which one's own intellectual traditions powerfully, although unconsciously, shape our concepts of training and ministry. For this reason, it is appropriate to greet each suggested goal with a "hermeneutic of suspicion." We might ask, "Is it really necessary for graduates to know this? Why is this needed? Which skill competency would graduates be unable to develop or demonstrate without this knowledge?" By testing each proposed knowledge goal against the specified competencies, the economy and focus of the seminary curriculum can be assured.

Skill development also requires practice or guided experience. In addition to listing knowledge needed to address competencies in the profile of an ideal graduate, the faculty also should consider experiential learning needed to achieve an appropriate level of proficiency in each skill area. Only as knowledge is combined with guided experience will needed skills be developed.

The faculty can be aided in this task by using Training Goals Worksheets (see Figure 7.1). For each skill area, specific competencies identified by the Stakeholders' Panel should be listed in the first column. In the second and third columns, faculty members can list knowledge and experience required to achieve and support the identified competency. The faculty's knowledge of Scripture, disciplinary literature, and supervised ministry opportunities are resources the faculty brings to this task. This step should be undertaken as a creative and interactive process engaged in by all members of the faculty. Only as the faculty applies its collective knowledge and wisdom to the task can it expect to arrive at training goals that are owned by the whole faculty and that serve well its graduates and its constituent ministries.

Training Goals Worksheet SKILL AREA: Interpersonal Relations		
Skill Competencies	**Required Knowledge [Information and Principles]**	**Required Experiences**
• Applies Biblical principles to relationships	• Doctrine of the image of God in humans • Matthew 5–7 • The relational patterns of Jesus • Romans 13–16 • 1 Corinthians	• Journaling on relational life on campus, in community, or in family • Small-group discussion of relationship information and principles, plus journal entries
• Listens and responds appropriately	• Principles of attentive listening • Principles of appropriate interaction	• Guided experience (e.g. role play or simulations) on attentive listening and appropriate interaction
• Manages interpersonal conflict well	• Joshua 22 • Matthew 18 • 1 Corinthians 6 • Conflict resolution strategies	• Guided experience (e.g. role play) on conflict resolution • Journaling on conflict and resolution on campus, in community, or in family

Figure 7.1: Training Goals Worksheet

Identify Knowledge That Fosters Needed Character Qualities

When knowledge and experiences needed to develop and support skill competencies have been identified, attention shifts to knowledge that can be expected to contribute to development of character qualities included in the profile. Although "experiences" also contribute to development of character, a caution is in order. We can plan and require experiences that develop skills (like role play and mentored engagement in ministry) but it is not appropriate for us to engineer experiences – such as stress or deprivation or failure – to develop character. That is the role of the Holy Spirit.

The relationship between knowledge and character is quite different from the relationship between knowledge and skills. Specific knowledge is needed to develop and perform any skill. Character, in contrast, is not a function of knowledge. Those with the greatest integrity, young children, for example, also may be the least knowledgeable. On the other hand, many have learned by sad experience that the most knowledgeable individuals sometimes are the least trustworthy. This warns us that asking, "What must a person know in order to be like this?" is not a useful way to proceed when identifying knowledge goals related to character qualities.

It often is said that character qualities are "better caught than taught," that is, they are best learned by reflection on living models. Knowledge of Scripture, however, is vital. The Holy Spirit uses the Scriptures to teach us God's standards for holy living and to hold before us the sinless life of Jesus, our ultimate example. Paul reminds us that the Old Testament histories are "written . . . for our instruction" (1 Cor 10:6, 11). Furthermore, God uses his Word as a channel to bring his grace into our lives. It "is useful for teaching, rebuking, correcting and training in righteousness" (2 Tim 3:16 NIV). Knowledge of historical models of godly character, as in the stories of saints and martyrs or in biographies of lay Christians, ministry leaders, and missionaries, also is useful. Thus, for each character quality listed, ask, "What knowledge is needed to reprove, to instruct, or to foster the development of this quality?"

Again, the critical term is "needed." This is not an opportunity to justify intellectual traditions or academic disciplines in which we are vested. This is not the time for a faculty member to smuggle into the curriculum areas of personal or professional interest. Knowledge goals should relate directly to character qualities. More useful questions may be, "What does the Bible teach regarding this character quality?" or "Where in the Scriptures is this quality demonstrated, either positively or negatively?" As with skill competencies, when identifying knowledge to develop any character quality, we should apply a "hermeneutic of suspicion."

Creating curriculum planning worksheets for every skill area and character quality area included in your program goals may take several months. It may be necessary to divide and delegate the task to cross-disciplinary work groups within the faculty but, in the end, it is important that the whole faculty reviews and approves the work of every work group. When curriculum planning worksheets have been prepared for all skill and quality areas, together they represent your "Training Goals."

Develop Courses That Address Needed Knowledge and Experience

When a graduate is able skillfully to employ the identified competencies and consistently to model the identified qualities, and is equipped with the knowledge needed to fulfill the envisioned ministry leadership role, the mission of the seminary has been fulfilled. Lists of competencies, qualities, and knowledge, however, are not a curriculum of studies. Dealing with fifteen or more curriculum planning worksheets (i.e. one for each general skill area and quality area in the profile) can be challenging. The faculty must develop a list of courses that address these training goals.

The task of developing courses to address training goals is more art than science. Working together, the faculty must identify discrete topics or themes reflected in the training goals. The challenge will be to conceive a list of courses that address all of our training goals and that can be taught within the time allotted for the program of study. Until all competencies, qualities, and knowledge identified has been assigned to one or more courses, the work of the faculty is not complete. We cannot lose track of any general or specific skill or character area that our training must develop if graduates are to reflect the profile required by our calling. Assigning a training goal to two or more courses is not a problem; repetition is an effective educational principle.

Much wisdom, insight, and grace is needed for a faculty to work together to identify courses and experiential learning requirements (i.e. supervised experiences in addition to those provided in courses) that will provide learners with the knowledge, skills, and character qualities needed to minister effectively. The faculty is wise to remind itself often during this process of the mission of the seminary and its collective calling to equip graduates for effective ministry leadership. Unless a faculty is unified in this commitment, developing a new curriculum can become polarizing, fracturing, and fragmenting. On the other hand, persevering together through the long and difficult process of developing a transformative, mission-centered curriculum can be a unifying experience for a faculty. It is for this reason that curriculum development should be pursued prayerfully and in dependence on the Holy Spirit.

Use a Matrix to Validate the New Curriculum

The concept of a curriculum matrix is simple and its use is not complicated. Because of the size of a curriculum matrix, it may be convenient to use computer spreadsheet software, even though a pen and ink matrix on newsprint or chart paper also is feasible.

The curriculum matrix simply is a grid with the program's training goals arrayed across the top and its curriculum of courses arrayed down the left side. A check mark is then inserted into each cell where the goals of a course include a specified training goal (see Figure 7.2). When the matrix is complete, the faculty easily can identify any training goal that has been slighted or overlooked. It also will be apparent if any course has been assigned an unreasonable number of training goals.

The sample curriculum matrix provided in Figure 7.2 lists a few courses that may be offered by an African seminary but does not specify the skill competencies, character qualities, or knowledge that comprise the training goals of this hypothetical seminary. Thus, the sample matrix is incomplete and only illustrative. In this illustration, however, the matrix reveals that Character Quality Goal 3 is addressed in only one course. It seems unlikely that that quality can be developed adequately with so little attention. On the other hand, Knowledge Goal 1 is addressed in most of the courses. Probably the attention

	Competency 1	Competency 2	Competency 3	Competency …	Quality 1	Quality 2	Quality 3	Quality …	Knowledge 1	Knowledge 2	Knowledge 3	Knowledge …
Old Testament Survey 1	✓		✓		✓				✓			
Old Testament Survey 2	✓					✓			✓	✓		✓
New Testament Survey 1	✓				✓				✓			
New Testament Survey 2	✓							✓	✓	✓		
Systematic Theology 1		✓			✓	✓			✓		✓	
Systematic Theology 2		✓				✓			✓			
Systematic Theology 3		✓				✓			✓			✓
Hermeneutics	✓				✓				✓			
History of the Church in Africa			✓					✓				
Islam in Africa		✓	✓						✓			
Baptist Distinctives			✓			✓			✓		✓	
African Social Realities		✓	✓									✓
The Christian Life	✓	✓			✓					✓	✓	
Evangelism & Church Growth			✓					✓				
Pastoral Theology			✓						✓		✓	
Biblical Counseling	✓		✓		✓		✓		✓			
…												

Figure 7.2: Sample Curriculum Matrix[2]

devoted to this goal could be reduced or even deleted from some courses with attention redirected toward other training goals.

In contrast, "History of the Church in Africa" and "Evangelism and Church Growth" each have been assigned only one skill competency goal, one character quality goal, and no knowledge goals. This may be appropriate but it is likely these courses could be assigned more of the skill, character, and knowledge goals needed to realize the seminary's mission. Alternatively, perhaps inclusion

---

2. Note that the ellipses (. . .) are intended to indicate that this sample matrix is incomplete. A typical seminary curriculum matrix may be thirty or more columns wide with a similar number of rows.

of these courses should be questioned, since they contribute so little that corresponds to the profile chart.

In addition to its application when developing a new curriculum, a curriculum matrix also can be used to assess the appropriateness of an existing curriculum. If training goals have been specified, the curriculum can be mapped to assess its strengths and weaknesses. Caution is appropriate, however, when employing a curriculum matrix to assess a curriculum that has been developed without first identifying the profile of an ideal graduate. A curriculum may address a seminary's stated training goals but if those goals were developed by the faculty without reference to the context and challenges of graduates in ministry, we simply have a closed, self-validating system that may be unrelated to the reality of graduates' ministries. This is why the role of the Stakeholders' Panel is critical to the integrity of curriculum development.

When the new curriculum has been mapped and requisite adjustments have been made, the curriculum development task is complete. It is appropriate to celebrate the achievement which God has enabled. Attention next shifts to the task of planning the courses prescribed in the curriculum we have developed.

8

Planning Courses for Transformative Learning

Developing a curriculum that equips the seminary's entering students to function in ministry is the first responsibility of the seminary's faculty. The faculty also must develop course syllabi and lesson plans that translate the curriculum into actionable plans of instruction, studies, and learning experiences that foster transformative learning.

One of the advantages of the approach to curriculum development we have described is that each course is required to occupy a specific place and to carry out a specific function in the curriculum of studies. Courses are selected and shaped not on the basis of tradition or disciplinary interests of faculty members but on the basis of institutional mission and specific learning required to realize that mission and calling.

As the curriculum is developed, each course is assigned training goals it is expected to address. This approach brings focus and discipline to the task of course development as well as to course evaluation. If students are not attaining the goals specified for a course, appropriate adjustments in course design and teaching–learning methods should be expected. Given the substantial discretion and lack of accountability faculty members often have enjoyed in the past, this may require an adjustment in thinking. Faculty members have a high sense of calling and a deep desire to see students' lives and ministries transformed by their courses. Adopting an approach to course design and teaching disciplined by course goals can equip graduates to see transformational change in the churches and communities they serve. This recognition is very motivating.

Creating Syllabi That Honor and Achieve Course Goals

Vella's "eight steps of planning"[1] is an invaluable guide to course design. Typically, our first question is "What is the content I must cover?" That question quickly becomes "What textbook should I use?" Vella cautions us, however, that responsible course design must begin with the "antecedent questions" *Who? Why?*, *When?*, and *Where?* Understanding our learners and the context and resources of our teaching–learning environment must shape our planning. If these students have been enrolled in previous courses we have taught, all that may be required is reflection on how their personalities and backgrounds relate to this course. If we do not know our learners personally, we may need to gather information to inform our course planning.

Vella's fifth step, *So that?*, reminds us that this course exists within a larger curriculum and that it is expected to address goals specified in that curriculum – the character qualities and skills to be developed in this course. If a curriculum matrix exists, it will provide an accessible guide to the goals assigned. The teacher's challenge is to develop a learning plan designed to achieve these goals in the lives of the students who enroll in this course.

Although we may be tempted to treat the goals assigned to our course in the curriculum as suggestions, none can be discarded without impacting the effectiveness of the curriculum. Similarly, care should be taken before individual faculty members elect to augment their courses with unassigned goals since those goals may affect the coherence and focus of the curricular design. Certainly, any change from assigned course goals should be approved by the faculty's curriculum committee or dean.

"So that?" also reminds us that assignment of goals should extend to each lesson in a course. How will each lesson contribute to developing the character qualities and skills assigned to this course? Lesson goals, of course, are more specific than course goals but, taken as a whole, lesson goals should insure that course goals will be realized. As we will see, lesson goals provide needed direction for lesson planning.

With our students, the context and resources of the teaching–learning environment, and the course goals in mind, we finally are ready to address

---

1. See the discussion of Vella's "eight steps of planning" in chapter 3 and elaboration of "the antecedent questions" in chapter 4.

the *What?* – the knowledge and understandings that undergird, develop, and support the character qualities and skills assigned as course goals. Some knowledge goals may be assigned to this course in the curriculum plan but opportunity also exists for teachers to select subject matter particularly appropriate to the development and prior experience of their students. All subject matter included in the course design should contribute to developing and supporting the assigned character qualities and skills. Any temptation to include more than is needed should be resisted, recalling the adult education principle that "less is more." Enabling our students to learn thoroughly must take priority over our personal scholarly interests or supplementary material we find interesting.

Reflecting on the antecedent questions and on course goals may lead to identifying "units," or topical segments, within the course plan. How will the course sessions be distributed among these units? How many classes will be assigned to each? In this way, a course calendar or course schedule begins to emerge. With the course schedule in hand, it is time to step back and ask, "Does this schedule afford confidence that the course goals can be realized in the time allocated? Is it realistic to assume that the information and learning experiences included in this course plan will develop and support the character qualities and skills assigned as goals for this course?" Only if the answer is "Yes" can we afford to move ahead in designing the course.

Vella offers a sage caution: "Remember: the danger is to design too much *what* for the *when*."[2] She advocates allowing margins, choosing to plan for less time than is allocated. She observes:

> No problem is so consistent as designing too much *what* for the *when*. How many times have you been at a training session or a course where the professor or instructor says, "We don't have enough time to do this thoroughly" or "If we only had enough time, we could do this well"? You will not hear those phrases in using this approach to learning-centered design, because here you design for the time you are given. You do it well – every time.[3]

---

2. Jane Vella, *Taking Learning to Task* (San Francisco: Jossey-Bass, 2001), 30.

3. Vella, *Taking Learning to Task*, 86.

Vella's seventh step, *What for?*, challenges the teacher to identify achievement objectives for this course. In chapter 3, we saw that achievement objectives state what learners *will have done* in order to assure themselves and others that they have learned. The italicized words are critically important. Achievement objectives do not specify what the teacher will do (although they bear significant implications for teaching priorities and strategies), nor do they describe what we expect learners will be able to do. Teaching–learning objectives cannot be about our hopes and aspirations for our students. Rather, achievement objectives describe what students will do in this course to experience and validate the learning envisioned in course goals.

If a course is expected to develop effectiveness in sharing the gospel, an achievement objective may be: "By the end of the course, each student will have shared the gospel message effectively with at least five non-Christians." The teacher's role is to prepare the student to share the gospel effectively, perhaps including role play and active coaching, but the achievement objective describes what the student will have done. If effectively sharing the gospel is a course goal, there can be no doubt whether that goal has been achieved when the student has done it. The same is true whether the achievement objective is exegeting a text, delivering a sermon, explaining a Bible truth so others understand clearly, sensitively confronting a cult member, comforting the bereaved, or challenging an oppressive relationship or structure. Achievement objectives are "tough" on teachers because they demand that we do our job well.[4] As such, they are our friends; they help us achieve our teaching–learning goals.

With clarity regarding our learners, the context and resources of our learning environment, the goals assigned to our course within the school's curriculum of studies, the knowledge, skills, and character qualities to be taught, and the achievement objectives that will insure learning, it is a short step to determining the *How?*, the teaching methods that will enable realization of the course achievement objectives. Indeed, methods typically can be recognized as implicit in well-framed achievement objectives.

This is the time for designing term projects, for identifying teaching resources and, possibly, for selecting a textbook. Any textbook must be appropriate to the course achievement objectives and may, therefore, be

---

4. Vella, 52.

difficult to find. If an inappropriate textbook is selected, it may divert the course away from achievement objectives that are appropriate to your students and context. No textbook, irrespective of the prestige in which it is held by others, is worth that price.

The syllabus is a course plan that summarizes your work. Typically, it will include the name and official description of the course as stated in the seminary's curriculum of studies. The course goals and achievement objectives should be listed so students will know what they will learn to be and do as a result of enrolling in this course. If students are expected to obtain a textbook or other supporting materials, instructions should be provided in the syllabus. The syllabus also should include a schedule of classes with the topic for the day and daily pre-class assignments clearly stated. It also is helpful to indicate due dates for term projects or out-of-class assignments on the schedule of classes. Finally, the syllabus should state how student learning will be assessed – criteria to be applied and the methods to be used. A syllabus that includes the information listed in this paragraph will function as a contract between the teacher and students. Students know what is expected of them and what they can expect of the teacher.

Designing Lesson Plans That Address Course Goals

Having developed a course plan and syllabus, designing a lesson plan involves the same process in miniature. Again, Vella's eight steps of planning are our guide. We recall the *Who?* and *Why?* of our students and confirm the specific *When?* and *Where?* of the lesson to be planned. The *So that?* of the lesson is the aim assigned when the course was planned; it locates the lesson within the larger landscape of the course.

The *What?* of the lesson is the specific knowledge that must be taught to develop and support in specific ways the skills and character qualities toward which the course is directed. Since we assume the lesson will be designed as a sequence of learning tasks and that learning will be active, employing multiple methods, the teacher must discern what knowledge is essential. Although there may be much more information that we find fascinating and want to share, we recall that instruction will be disciplined by learning tasks and that a common fault of adult educators is attempting to teach "too much *what* for the *when*."

We may find this forced selectivity painful but we know it facilitates learning among our students.

Stating achievement objectives, the *What for?* of the lesson continues the discipline over our instincts and habits that the "eight steps of planning" impose. Typically, it is much easier to state what I will do (i.e. a teaching objective) or what I expect and hope learners will be able to do (i.e. a behavioral objective) than to state what my learners will do to demonstrate they have learned what I have taught (i.e. an achievement objective).

The verbs chosen to state the achievement objectives must be "tough." If we expect learners to demonstrate learning, verbs must describe observable actions. State of being verbs, like "will be," and verbs that describe characteristics, like "will understand," are not useful when stating achievement objectives. Action verbs, like "will identify," "will explain," "will recite," or "will illustrate," serve much better.[5]

Taken as a set, achievement objectives stated for this lesson should thoroughly address the aims of the lesson within the broader context of the course. No lesson should be expected to address all course goals but each lesson must contribute to achievement of those goals. If one realizes that achievement objectives indicated by the lesson aim are unrealistic within the time available, it will be necessary to revisit the course design. Teachers need to attempt less in order to achieve more. When we sacrifice pedagogic rigor in the interest of unrealistic goals, student learning suffers.

It is worth recalling that the *How?*, the learning tasks, typically are implicit in well-designed achievement objectives. Since "a learning task is an open question put to learners who have all the resources they need to respond,"[6] planning learning tasks necessarily includes insuring that learners have the resources needed to complete the assigned task successfully.

A variety of teaching methods can be used to insure that learners have the needed resources. Pre-class reading assignments, pre-class research in the community, pre-class or in-class inductive or exegetical Bible studies, brief lectures, video clips, case studies, reports on research findings, and

---

5. Vella (49–57) insists that verbs in achievement objectives should be "tough, productive, and respectful."
6. Vella, 8.

many other creative methods can be chosen to insure that learners have the needed information.

The learning task, however, requires learners to apply that information in order to demonstrate they have learned it. The in-class task assigned may entail individual reflection and journaling, role play, small-group work, "buzz group" sharing or discussion in twos or threes, large-group discussions, or spontaneous or structured debate. In-class learning tasks may be supplemented and supported by out-of-class mentoring and in-ministry group or individual projects and assignments. There are many ways to enable learners to demonstrate that they are equipped for ministry, that they have acquired the skills and developed the character qualities we teach. There is no need for learning in our classrooms to be boring!

Teaching for Life and Ministry Transformation

As we teach, it is important constantly to keep before us the goals we pursue – both our ultimate goal and the immediate goal of this lesson. The ultimate goal we have proposed is transformation of the church and society through the power of God's Word and Spirit. The means to that goal is seminary graduates who themselves have been transformed through obedience to the Word taught and who have been equipped to lead their churches and parachurch ministries as agents of God's transforming power.

The immediate goal of a lesson may be less grand but is more urgent. Every lesson is a building block that contributes to – or diminishes – realization of the greater goal. That being so, we need to be clear regarding our task as facilitators of God's transforming work in our students. The immediate goals of our lessons will vary according to the achievement objectives for the lesson. Whatever our achievement objectives, however, we do well to fix clearly in mind what we ask God to accomplish in our learners through this lesson. A helpful way to express this is to ask, "What is the goal toward which we teach?" or "What are we teaching toward?"

Duane and Muriel Elmers' "Cycle of Learning"[7] can be most helpful in this regard. There are times when it is completely appropriate to "teach toward"

---

7. See chapter 4 for a discussion of the Elmers' "Cycle of Learning."

simple *recall*. Memorization of Scripture is a valid and valuable teaching goal. The psalmist sings, "I have stored up your word in my heart, that I might not sin against you" (Ps 119:11). Consider, also, memorization of the order of books of the Bible. If they were arranged alphabetically, it would not be necessary to memorize the order of the Bible's books. Since they are not alphabetical, memorization of the order of the books of the Bible enables us to find passages quickly. There are many learning goals that can best be achieved by teaching toward recall.

At other times, our teaching goal may be *recall with appreciation*. Again, the psalmist sings, "Oh how I love your law! It is my meditation all the day" (Ps 119:97). Our desire as teachers is that our students also will love God's law. It is appropriate, therefore, for some lessons to be taught toward that goal. There are other "affects," or "values," or "heart responses" that we may teach toward at times. Teaching toward motivation to action, to obedience, to faithfulness, to boldness, to endurance, or to faith in God are important goals, any one of which may be the appropriate goal of a lesson. The Elmers remind us that conviction is a powerful heart response. Perhaps as you pray for your students, you will teach lessons in which you pray God will convict them by his Spirit and that becomes the goal you teach toward.

In many of our lessons, the goal will be to lead learners to *recall with speculation*, looking ahead to imagine ways the truth learned may be applied in their lives, their families, communities, or ministries. Our goal is to lead learners to obedience to God's truth but imagining specific and concrete ways to obey is a positive step toward obedience. Recall with speculation also intentionally anticipates barriers to obedience and visualizes strategies for overcoming those barriers. Our fallen nature and Satan's stratagems design to keep us from obeying God and the truth he has revealed. Unless we teach toward recall with speculation, few of our students will move from good intentions to disciplined and joyful obedience. Teaching toward recall with speculation may be the most important gift we can give to our students.

Speculation regarding obedience has value, however, only as it leads to *recall with application*. Loving God with our heart, mind, and strength gains worth only when it leads to transformed behaviors, relationships, and priorities. Although this is a goal toward which we teach, we typically get only glimpses of it in the classroom. Disciplined obedience is more recognizable on campus or in community. Mentoring programs, on campus and in ministry, often afford a window into learners' commitment to obey God's truth. When trust between teachers and learners is high, an assignment for students to journal also may provide opportunities to observe our students' choices to obey truths discussed in our classes.

Our ultimate goal is *recall with integration*, to see the truth we teach so deeply woven into the values and life-ways of our students that these truths shape and determine their natural response. Since this can be observed only in alumni with established families and ministries, recall with integration most often will be a prayer goal, rather than a teaching goal. Nevertheless, it is appropriate for learners to know that we pray the truths we teach will find a permanent place in their lives. Ultimately, this is what we teach toward in all that we do. Clarity regarding the ultimate and immediate goals of the lessons we teach is an invaluable discipline as we teach for life and ministry transformation.

Caution

The approach to course design and lesson preparation described in this chapter may be persuasive but implementation will be demanding. If all of your courses are new or if, in one term, you decide you will redesign all the courses you currently teach to employ dialogical learning principles, you quickly will be overwhelmed. Failure easily could lead to cynicism regarding the possibility and value of transformative teaching and learning. The reason for the failure, however, is not the usefulness of the methods we have described but rather the unrealistic scope of the task attempted.

If all courses you are assigned to teach are new, it will be critically important to insure that each course is designed using Vella's eight steps of planning, with specific goals designated for each lesson. If you teach a full-time course load, you probably will not be able to design creative, interactive learning plans for each lesson in the first year. In that case, it is wise to identify lessons that are most important to the goals of each course and to prioritize designing interactive lesson plans for those lessons. For other lessons, you may choose to lecture during the initial year, understanding that designing interactive plans for those lessons will be prioritized in the following year.

If the courses you are assigned to teach will not change but you now recognize the value of teaching interactively, teaching toward transformation rather than only toward transfer of information, the task is still huge. Attempting to revise all course and lesson plans in one term is not realistic. A better strategy is to work on redesigning only one or two courses each term, gradually encountering and conquering the challenges of dialogue education.

As you hone your skills as a learning facilitator, this will come more naturally. It is normal to find the rigors of dialogue education initially challenging. Don't give up. The change in your classroom and in your learners that results from your disciplined persistence will be deeply rewarding. Many faculty members in diverse cultural and ministry settings testify to the validity of the principles of planning for transformational teaching and learning described in these chapters.

9

Assessing Ministry Education

Assessment of teaching and learning is critical to stewardship of our ministry as teachers and as seminaries. Teachers need to know which of their teaching resources and methods are most effective and helpful to students. Administrators need to be assured that courses taught are well aligned with the values of the seminary and achieve the goals prescribed in the school's curriculum. Course assessment can provide valuable guidance in the professional development of faculty members.

Assessment also is critically important, both internally and externally, at the institutional level. Well-designed and well-executed institutional assessment validates the appropriateness of the seminary's instructional programs or alerts faculty and administrators to areas of needed improvement. Institutional assessment also assures the seminary's stakeholders that their needs are well served or, if findings are disappointing, that more fundamental change may be needed in the school's programs or leadership. Institutional assessment also assures donors that their support is appropriately directed and well stewarded.

Although specific approaches to assessment provide insight into various aspects of the life of the seminary, the most insightful institutional assessment examines a seminary's social impact. Seminaries exist to equip students for ministry. If asked why equipping students is important, we note that churches and parachurch ministries need effective, biblically qualified leaders. If asked why churches and parachurch ministries need qualified leaders, we affirm God's calling and mission to evangelism, discipleship, and church growth. Ultimately, however, God's desire is communities in which righteousness and justice reign, in which God is glorified, and in which the needy and hurting receive compassionate care. The effect of evangelism, discipleship, and church-growth ministries should be evident in our congregations and communities.

Impact assessment examines a seminary's effectiveness in bringing transformational change to the churches and communities served by its graduates. If students score high marks in examinations and graduates quickly find places of ministry but the churches where graduates serve are torn by dissension, are crippled by disengagement from their communities, or have little effect on the moral and spiritual quality of those they touch, neither the seminary nor its stakeholders should be satisfied that it fulfills its mission and calling.

The Evolution of Assessment Foci

Only recently have evaluators looked for evidence of institutional impact. Informal (and undocumented) approaches to institutional assessment have long taken the form of comparing one institution with another. College administrators, faculties, alumni, and students may ask, "How does education at our school compare with that at another – at Oxford, at Harvard, or at a regionally recognized standard bearer?" With the emergence of peer accreditation agencies at the beginning of the twentieth century, focus shifted to assessing institutional resources and processes.[1] Accreditors asked, "What qualifications are held by members of the faculty?" "How many courses are required for a degree?" "How many books are available in the library?" "How adequately do the school's facilities support its educational programs?" In the 1980s, attention turned to outcomes, and more recently to outputs, of a school's educational programs.[2] Thus, accreditors and governmental regulatory and funding entities most frequently ask, "What is the graduation rate of incoming students?" "What evidence indicates that a school's stated educational and

---

1. Elaine El-Khawas, *Accreditation in the USA: Origins, Developments, and Future Prospects* (Paris: International Institute for Educational Planning, UNESCO, 2001), 27, accessed 27 July 2017, http://unesdoc.unesco.org/images/0012/001292/129295e.pdf.

2. Peter T. Ewell, "An Emerging Scholarship: A Brief History of Assessment" (paper, National Center for Higher Education Management Systems [NCHEMS]), 5, accessed 29 July 2017, https://westmoreland.edu/media/124908/ie-assessment-info-6-a_brief_history_of_assessment.pdf.

program goals are achieved in the experience of graduates?" "What is the average time required for graduates to attain professional certification or to find a position in their desired profession?" "What percentage of graduates are admitted to graduate study programs?"

More recently, educational assessment theorists and administrators have taken note of efforts in the philanthropic and nonprofit sectors to look beyond resources, processes, outputs, and outcomes to social impact.[3] If an institution has excellent facilities, highly qualified faculty, gifted students, and vocationally successful alumni but the families, organizations, and communities where graduates live and work are racked by conflict, violence, injustice, moral decay, and declining quality of life, can the college or university be considered successful? Social impact is especially critical for theological schools, where spiritual, moral, and relational impact is paramount.

Institutional Mission and Impact Assessment

Impact assessment begins with a disciplined review of an institution's mission statement. As we have seen, it is helpful for a board to ask, "To what has God called us?" "What is the specific contribution for which we are accountable as God advances his kingdom and grows his church?"

When considering the seminary's mission, it may be insightful to identify the places of service of graduates who graduated six to fifteen years previously.[4] What proportion are engaged in vocational or bi-vocational ministry? Where are they serving? What fruit exists from their ministries? To what extent does this evidence correspond to the board's sense of the seminary's calling? If evidence regarding the service and ministry impact of the seminary's alumni diverges from the board's sense of God's calling, what response is indicated? Is God prompting the board to reexamine its understanding of the seminary's mission or is he indicating that the administration and faculty must bring the school's programs into alignment with its mission?

---

3. The theme of the 2015 ICETE Consultation was "The Impact of Theological Education."
4. Many of those who graduated within the previous five years may still be adapting to ministry; those who graduated more than fifteen years previously, on the other hand, may not have been shaped by current curricula or faculty.

A useful mission statement is a prayerfully conceived expression of the board's sense of God's calling for the seminary. Typically, it will be visionary and faith-challenging, but specific and – with God's enablement – attainable. It will include not only impact of training on the lives of graduates but also the impact of graduates' ministries on the congregations and communities in which they serve.

Impact Assessment's "Logic Chain"

A helpful approach to assessing "impact" recognizes a "chain" of five links (Figure 9.1). Adapting the language of systems analysis, assessment theorists identify critical impact variables as "inputs," "activities," "outputs," "outcomes," and "impact."[5]

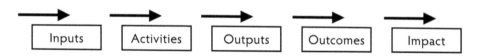

Figure 9.1: Impact Assessment Logic Chain

Inputs refers to resources available for pursuit of the seminary's mission, including the prior experiences of its students. *Activities* are the explicit and implicit curricula of the seminary, all that is done intentionally or otherwise to shape students and graduates. *Outputs* are the seminary's graduates, with the character qualities, skills, and knowledge they acquired as a result of their experiences through the seminary. *Outcomes* are the lives and ministries of those graduates as they live and minister in the places to which God leads them. And *Impact* is the effect of graduates' lives and ministries in the congregations and communities where they serve.

Each link in the impact logic chain is contingent on the one that precedes it. Thus, if inputs are limited, activities will be affected accordingly, and so on. If research indicates that a seminary's impact is different from its perceived

---

5. M. J. Epstein and K. Yuthas, *Measuring and Improving Social Impacts* (San Francisco: Barrett-Koehler, 2014).

mission, review of the logic chain can identify points of inadequacy or of mistaken assumptions.

Organizing for Impact Assessment

Assessment of a seminary's impact may be mandated by its board or initiated by administrators but leadership should be provided by the president, principal, or rector. He or she should appoint a team or task force to design a plan for assessing the seminary's impact, for collecting and analyzing needed data, and for reporting to the seminary's administration and board. This is a challenging task; without an impact-focused mission statement, it is impossible.

The first task of the impact assessment team is to construct a "logic chain." The impact-focused mission statement is the final link in the chain. Realistic descriptions of the seminary's resources and facilities, the experience and expertise of its faculty, its network of related congregations and communities, and the qualities and experience of incoming students constitute the seminary's "Inputs" link. The "Activities" link will note the explicit and implicit curricula and programs of the seminary. The "Outputs" link should include both the seminary's quantitative goals (i.e. the annual number of graduates) and its qualitative goals (i.e. the character, skill, and knowledge goals of each program). The "Outcomes" link may be the most critical, since it envisions means by which graduates will minister in order to effect change toward ends envisioned in the seminary's mission statement.

The "impact chain" is useful only as it is validated and owned by the seminary's major stakeholders. Members of the board, administration, and faculty must own the "impact chain" for impact assessment to have the institutional commitment and resources demanded by a disciplined and credible study. Validation of the "impact chain," however, is best provided by the seminary's external stakeholders, specifically its alumni and the church and parachurch ministries it exists to serve.[6]

While a school's impact logic chain typically is identified by an internal team or task force, it is prudent to ask external stakeholders to validate each

---

6. The "Stakeholders' Panel" employed in developing or revising the school's curricula can serve this purpose.

link in our logic chain. Thus, we may ask, "If we provide these activities – programs, courses, and community life practices – is it realistic to assume we can graduate persons who evidence the character qualities, skill competencies, and knowledge needed to minister effectively?" "If we facilitate the development of such graduates, is it realistic to assume they will provide effective leadership for the church and parachurch ministries the seminary intends to serve?" And "If these graduates minister as envisioned, is it realistic to assume the churches and communities in which they serve will be changed by the power of the Word and the Spirit, that broken relationships will be healed, that evil will be resisted, and that righteousness, justice, and compassion will thrive?" These are challenging questions which external stakeholders are better able to answer than is a school's faculty or administrators.

Once the "logic chain" is validated, inputs, activities, and outputs can be assessed using data readily available or easily collected in the seminary. These data typically are used by accrediting agencies to demonstrate the adequacy of the seminary's programs. Research on a seminary's outcomes is more complex. It will entail surveys and interviews of the seminary's alumni and of their parishioners and co-workers.

Research on impact is the most challenging; it rarely can be quantified. A seminary's impact can be uncovered only by using qualitative methods (e.g. direct observation, interviews, focus groups, case studies). Reliance on quantitative data tends to displace focus from impact to outputs. While a "snapshot" of a seminary's impact may be obtained through a time-limited project, a longitudinal study, comparing observations gathered over a period of years, will offer more robust findings and will reflect changes over time in the impact of the seminary and its graduates. When expedient, output and outcome data can serve as proxies for impact data provided the "logic chain" is endorsed by major stakeholders and conclusions are confirmed by disciplined observation and participant testimonies.

The purpose of impact assessment is not only to deliver a judgment on the seminary's success or failure with respect to its mission statement. The impact assessment report also should identify each link in the seminary's impact logic chain, noting factors that contribute positively or negatively to realization of mission and identifying opportunities for impact enhancement.

The Impact Logic Chain and Strategic Planning

The impact logic chain also is an effective tool for strategic planning. It is useful not only for summative evaluation, assessing the effectiveness of a program or its sponsoring institution, but also for formative evaluation, identifying areas of strength or needed improvement.

As already noted, each link in the logic chain is contingent on the one that precedes it. Therefore, working backwards, planners might ask, "How must graduates minister and relate to their congregations and communities in order to realize the impact mission envisioned for our seminary?" "What character qualities and ministry competencies must graduates evidence in order to minister in these ways?" "What kind of culture and activities must we provide in order to cultivate in graduates these qualities and competencies?" And finally, "How can available resources be deployed to support the needed activities?"

Employed as a strategic planning exercise, the impact logic chain can help planners be realistic as well as visionary. By focusing on social impact, planners can anticipate the potential for achieving an institution's mission – its calling from God. Furthermore, if there are breaks in the logic chain, planners can identify the factors that must be strengthened to attain or restore missional impact.

The contingency relationship between links alerts planners to limitations which must be accepted or addressed. If planners conclude that the stated mission of the seminary is unattainable given available inputs, the board may choose prayerfully to revisit its understanding of God's calling. As Hudson Taylor observed, "God's work done in God's way will never lack God's supplies."[7] Alternatively, the board may choose to provide additional resources or to appoint leadership that can employ available resources more creatively.

The Urgency of Impact Assessment

Impact assessment is important because the purpose of ministry education is not academic achievement or ordination qualification. God calls his people and his church to join him in his mission of reconciliation and extension of his

---

7. Cited in Leslie T. Lyall, *A Passion for the Impossible: The Continuing Story of the Mission Hudson Taylor Began* (London: OMF, 1965), 37.

kingdom. For too long, ministry educators have assumed that carefully crafted lectures will form graduates who minister effectively. By God's grace, some do. This is more likely, however, when seminaries aim for transformation of students' lives and ministries, for obedience to truths taught rather than only for transfer of information about the Bible and ministry functions. Impact assessment can encourage and can validate a seminary's focus on effective pursuit of God's calling.

10

The Challenge of Transforming Ministry Education

In this book we have argued that the task of ministry education is to equip leaders for Christ's church who are transformed by the power of the Word and the Spirit. For seminaries to graduate students who simply are *informed* by transfer of biblical, theological, and pastoral information does not equip them to lead their congregations to transformed lives. This is possible only as leaders themselves have been powerfully changed in likeness and obedience to Christ and thus are able to reproduce their own transformation in the lives of others.

Almost every evangelical seminary and faculty member would affirm this aspiration, yet current experience far too often appears different. In chapter 1, we noted changes that are needed for ministry education to achieve transformative impact. These changes will not come easily. Often, it seems, value patterns and practices that run counter to these principles are present in the culture of the church and in the culture of seminary education. Culture is not amenable to mandated change.[1] Nevertheless, change is possible, and – for

---

1. Organizational culture has been defined as "deeply embedded patterns of organizational behavior and the shared values, assumptions, beliefs, or ideologies that members have about their organization or its work" (M. Peterson and M. Spencer, cited by Susan M. Awbrey, "General Education Reform as Organizational Change: Integrating Cultural and Structural Change," *Journal of General Education* 54, no. 1 [2005]: 5). Change decrees may evoke superficial compliance but they do not alter deeply embedded behaviors and convictions. If these are unchanged, decreed changes soon will be subverted.

the sake of the church and God's global mission – urgent. At least three issues demand our attention.

Repurposing Ministry Education to Serve the Church

Seminary boards, their sponsoring churches, and seminary faculties and administrators affirm that the seminary exists to serve the church. Although lip service to this commitment is widespread, current realities point to a different conclusion. The values that shape seminary culture and life too often orient to the university, rather than to the church. Accreditation structures, whose approval seminaries work so hard to acquire and maintain, typically reflect the values of academe. Pursuit and extension of knowledge, rather than forming character and equipping for ministry, is most highly valued in the university. Elitism thrives in communities that prize academic titles and rituals, where students and faculty are ranked, where achievement is selectively celebrated, and where relationships are formal and, too often, distant. Individual effort and competition for recognition and rewards is endemic in academe. None of these values corresponds to a biblical vision of the church.

Seminary boards and faculties must allow biblical teaching on spiritual leadership to shape their curricula and their community life. The church must be given voice as a partner, rather than merely as a potential employer, in defining the scope, content, and context of ministry education. Engagement with the Scriptures cannot be "dumbed down" but critical wrestling with God's truth must be oriented – intentionally, relentlessly, and creatively – to transformation of the learner's life and ministry. Students must be led to obey – not only to recall – the truth they study. Only as students' lives are transformed by God and his Word can they lead others to Christlike lives of obedience that bring transformation to their churches and communities. In this book we have proposed and illustrated methods for realizing this repurposing.

Reshaping Faculty Selection, Development, and Rewards

The task of renewing ministry education is complicated by incumbent faculty structures. Proposals to reorient seminary education to the church, to recast faculty members as life and ministry role models, to redesign seminary curricula and instruction toward life transformation, and to employ participative and interactive methods of teaching are unnerving to many faculty members. They know they can succeed in a traditional seminary environment. If the rules change so radically, however, they have no confidence they will be able to survive, much less excel.

The changes we propose also may appear unfair to current members of the seminary faculty. Most were trained and selected as scholars who excel in an academic environment. Their primary areas of expertise are research and writing. They have learned that maintaining a significant power-distance relationship with students and those outside the academy enhances their credibility and wins prestige. Very few have encountered a teacher who taught interactively. Their most highly esteemed professors were lecturers, so they find it difficult to visualize themselves teaching any other way. Because they were hired as scholars and lecturers, it seems unfair to impose different expectations now. Reluctance – even resistance – from faculty members should be expected.

Assumptions evident in their hiring also are buttressed by the seminary's approach to faculty development. As at secular universities, seminary faculty development programs typically afford opportunities to engage in research or to write for scholarly publication. It is a rare seminary that assigns a faculty member to spend a semester immersed in congregational ministry or in cross-cultural discipleship. Like secular universities, seminaries tend to promote scholarly rather than spiritual, ministerial, or andragogic development of their faculty. It is natural, therefore, for faculty members to resist calls for change. They may feel they have been misdirected by past professional development priorities if the seminary pivots toward transformative teaching and learning.

The typical seminary's reward structure also supports the values and expectations of academe. Professorships, salary, and (in some contexts) tenure are tied to achievement portfolios judged by university standards. Suddenly, it may seem, faculty members find themselves confronted by a shift in values in which formerly prized achievements no longer have currency. Given the new expectations, their prospects for recognition or advancement may appear dubious. This, too, raises fears and prompts resistance.

The seminary cannot afford to lose its faculty members; the knowledge and skills they possess are critical to the future of the school. Clearly, retraining faculty members must be assigned high priority if the seminary is to pursue a transformative mission. Managing the fears, expectations, and development of members of the seminary faculty is a central and crucial aspect of transition from incumbent patterns of seminary training to ministry education that truly is transformative, characterized by new and life-changing ways of thinking, valuing, and relating to God and others.

Re-Forming Student and Stakeholder Expectations

One of the most challenging barriers to change is expectations shaped by the centuries-old history of ministry education. Tragically, in the late Middle Ages, ministry education divided into monastic and scholastic streams. Those two streams diverged and the scholastic tradition came to dominate ministerial education. By the time Calvin established his school in Geneva, virtually all Catholic priests were trained in cathedral schools that adhered to the scholastic model. Many cathedral schools evolved into universities. Preparation of ministers for the church was a principal motivation in founding Europe's and North America's oldest universities.

Throughout this history, theological schools and seminaries have focused on introducing students to a curriculum of theological knowledge and classic disciplines in keeping with the scholastic model. Emphasis is placed on the student encountering and mastering knowledge of the disciplines studied. The vast majority of today's ministers have been educated in this way. That's what seminary is, and seminary is the pathway to preparation and qualification for vocational ministry. It's what is expected by students and churches.

Furthermore, students expect their seminary experience will be much like their undergraduate experience. They expect to receive lectures from faculty members who are expert scholars and to be assigned books to read and papers to write. They also expect the academic skills they have honed during their university training to insure status and success at seminary and to privilege them in qualifying for placement in church and parachurch ministry positions.

Donors who support theological seminaries are conditioned to derive satisfaction from the quality of their school's faculty, from books authored by faculty members, from beautiful campus facilities, and from the number and esteem of their seminary's graduates. We should not be surprised if they do not welcome the suggestion that programs they have supported must be radically adapted to better serve the advance of Christ's kingdom.

Transformational ministry education challenges many of these expectations. Although the seminary campus remains the center for ministry preparation, classes are interactive and reflective, focused on character formation and obedience to biblical truth. Teachers relate to students as models and mentors more than as disciplinary scholars. Curricula include out-of-class, in-ministry, and in-community experiences which are valued as highly as classroom and individual studies. Because program goals are expressed in terms of character and ministry-skills formation, academic prowess does not guarantee success. Some students, faculty members, and donors, recognizing these priorities, will choose traditional over transformational approaches to ministry education.

Leading Institutional Change

John Kotter and William Bridges are among the most frequently cited organizational change theorists. Kotter's *Leading Change*[2] and its sequel, *The Heart of Change*,[3] prescribe an eight-stage strategy for effecting organizational change.[4] In *The Heart of Change*, Kotter emphasizes that change occurs as organizational members "see and feel" the need for change.[5]

In *Managing Transitions*,[6] Bridges identifies three phases of organizational change, with alternative roles for the leader in each phase. The phases are concurrent but the proportion of an organization's membership in each phase shifts as organizational change is adopted. Initially, a majority of the organization's members are occupied with "ending," releasing perspectives, patterns, and relationships familiar in the past. Gradually, a majority move to "the neutral zone" in which the old has been released but the new has not yet

---

2. John Kotter, *Leading Change* (Boston: Harvard Business School, 1996).

3. John Kotter, *The Heart of Change* (Boston: Harvard Business School, 2002).

4. Kotter's eight stages are: (1) Increase urgency; (2) Build a guiding team; (3) Identify an uplifting vision; (4) Communicate the vision; (5) Remove barriers to success; (6) Create short-term wins; (7) Persist; and (8) Nurture a new culture. Kotter acknowledges that the "stages" may sequence differently in some contexts but argues that all are important to effect lasting organizational change (Kotter, *Heart of Change*, 6–7).

5. Kotter, *Heart of Change*, 7.

6. William Bridges, *Managing Transitions* (Cambridge, MA: Da Capo Press, 1991, 2003).

become routine. Organizational change is complete only when a significant majority have embraced the change, evidenced by new patterns of thought and behavior.

Although Kotter and Bridges employ alternative images of the organizational change process, the advice they offer is largely congruent. Both organizational change literature and our own experience lead us to urge church leaders and theological educators to pursue an approach to culture change in theological seminaries that, in turn, can lead to transformational change in the life and ministry of Christ's church.

Cultivate Shared Commitment to Transformational Ministry Education

Change in the cultures of church and seminary cannot be realized through the efforts of individual leaders. Many – often referred to as "a critical mass" – must recognize that the status quo is unacceptable, that change is essential.[7] This process must be bathed in prayer for God's will to be made clear and for God's people to align themselves with his vision for his church.

The Scriptures clearly teach that God desires his church to experience holiness of life – individual and corporate (Matt 5:48; 1 Pet 1:14–16). This is only possible as we allow God to transform our worldview, our perspectives, values, and priorities. Lack of holiness among Christians does not reflect any deficiency in God's grace, but only our failure to allow God to change us, conforming our thoughts and behaviors to those of Christ.

God desires us to hate sin and to love righteousness as he does. He calls us to simplicity of life and stewardship of wealth for ministry to others. He expects us to love fellow-Christians and to be compassionate to all who suffer and are oppressed. So often our lives as Christians are indistinguishable from those of our non-Christian neighbors. We have so many ways to justify our self-absorption, our pursuit of things and wealth, our deflection of the pain of those around us. We preach that none is perfect except God and fail to mention that Jesus urges us to obey God's commands, aligning our lives with his (Matt

---

7. Kotter advises change leaders to "increase urgency" (*Heart of Change*, 15–36) and Bridges urges change leaders to "sell the problem that is the reason for the change" (*Managing Transitions*, 16).

19:17). We offer theological excuses for our failure to experience what God desires, commands, and offers to us. How long will he be patient with us?

God intends his church to be a "light to the nations." He taught us to pray, "Your kingdom come, your will be done, on earth as it is in heaven" (Matt 6:10). Throughout the Scriptures, God's intention for all people is that they would enter his *shalom* – to experience life as he intends. *Shalom* is completely foreign to the state of our world, of our nations, and of our communities. Satan is effectively shaping our communities and our culture in evil and destructive ways. The church too rarely engages in this spiritual battle for righteousness, justice, and compassion. How can we be satisfied to meet in our churches, singing praise songs and celebrating or debating points of theology, when God weeps over our communities and our nations (Matt 23:37)?

Why is it that the watching world, observing the life of the church, so rarely acknowledges the amazing beauty and holiness of our God (Matt 5:16)? Why is the global church so spiritually immature and its influence in the communities and cultures of this world so impotent? That is not what God intends. His intention is that the mutual ministry of believers to one another will lead to full spiritual maturity – the spiritual maturity of Jesus Christ (Eph 4:12–13). It is for this reason that the Holy Spirit distributes various capacities for ministry among God's people (1 Cor 12:7–11). It is for this purpose he sends us into the world as his witnesses (Acts 1:8).

To be effective, however, Christians must be equipped to exercise their God-given capacities. For that purpose the risen Christ gives to the church leaders who can equip believers for ministries of sharing the good news, ministering across cultural barriers, insightfully declaring God's message to those inside and outside the church, and shepherding and teaching God's people (Eph 4:11). When church leaders do not equip believers for ministry to one another, the church stagnates. Its ministry of preserving morality and shining God's truth into surrounding communities and cultures is muted (Matt 5:13).

Seminaries and theological colleges are entrusted with the task of preparing leaders for Christ's church – those who will equip believers for their diverse ministries. When seminaries focus on transferring information, however, graduates conceive their role the same way. Rather than obeying God's truth and being transformed by the power of the Word and the Spirit, believers are informed about things they need to know. Rather than being equipped for their mutual ministry of maturing, witnessing, and serving, believers are given information, just as their leaders were given information in seminary, with the assumption that they will know how to apply it – and will do so.

God's normal means of bringing spiritual life to his people is godly leaders – men and women whose minds and hearts have been transformed by the power of the gospel, whose lives reflect God's perspectives and priorities. Rather than being institutions wittingly or unwittingly occupied with transfer of information, our seminaries must be seminal communities[8] where lives and ministries are transformed by the Holy Spirit in personal encounter with God's Word. Then leaders, thus transformed, can extend this same transformation to the congregations and communities where they serve.

Only as seminary boards, administrators, and faculties recognize the critical failure of the church in the world, and their complicity in the ineffectiveness of the church and its leadership, will they find the will to change.

Enlist the Partnership of the Constituent Church

The seminary cannot navigate this transition alone. It needs the collaboration and support of its constituent church. This will not be easy to obtain because seminaries, for centuries, have portrayed themselves as repositories of technical and ministry expertise. Our constituent churches accept and respect that expertise and thus find it difficult to believe they possess wisdom needed by seminary faculties.

Faculties do, of course, possess important expertise – in scholarly research, theology, biblical studies, church history, and in ministry theories and strategies – but the church also has knowledge needed by the seminary. The church understands from daily experience the cultural, social, and relational challenges faced by Christians. The church understands the barriers to Christian witness and how witness is received or rejected by neighbors, friends, and colleagues. The church understands how non-Christian neighbors respond to efforts to initiate spiritual conversations – what enables spiritual conversations and what closes them. This knowledge is needed by the seminary if leaders are to be prepared for effectiveness in ministry. This is

---

8. The etymological derivation of the word "seminary" is from the Latin "seedbed."

why curriculum development must be undertaken collaboratively with the seminary's stakeholders.

The seminary also needs to establish partnership with the church because redesigning the seminary for transformational teaching and learning is not an end in itself. The end goal is transformed believers and congregations. As the church participates in rethinking and redesigning ministry education, it can see and appreciate God's intention for his church.

Provide Retooling and Support for the Seminary Faculty

It is neither fair nor realistic to expect faculty members to abandon familiar models of teaching and to adopt new models without training that includes demonstration and practice. Transformational teaching and learning is very different from and more demanding than the educational models most seminary faculty members have experienced or practiced. Not all faculty members will welcome this training. Experience demonstrates, however, that those who once were most resistant – even dismissive – can become passionate advocates of participative learning and facilitative teaching perspectives and skills.

In addition to professional development training, the seminary also needs to provide faculty members with appropriate support during the transition to new roles. Reorientation of the seminary to provide transformational ministry preparation cannot be achieved in a day, a term, or a year. Faculty members can immediately redirect their teaching toward obedience to, rather than only toward recall of, God's truth. Restructuring of syllabi and lesson plans toward participative learning, however, will take longer. This is demanding work. Most faculty members will find they realistically can recreate only one course each term. Ownership and excitement will build, however, as each newly redesigned course is celebrated by the seminary's entire faculty.

Recognize That Transition Is a Process That Entails Loss

Bridges employs the metaphor of the exodus of Jews from Egypt to illustrate the psychological and emotional toll of organizational change. First Moses had to get Egypt out of the Jews – they had to leave Egypt emotionally, as well as physically – before he could get the Jews into the promised land.[9] Bridges

---

9. Bridges, *Managing Transitions*, 64.

makes the point that people typically do not resist change; what they resist is loss.[10]

The losses experienced by faculty members transitioning to transformational teaching methods are daunting. Overnight, courses in which they have invested years of professional engagement may become obsolete. Skills they have developed as lecturers diminish in value. Topics of professional interest and scholarly pursuit may find little or no place in a curriculum reoriented to developing character and ministry skills. In addition, they lose the buffering from the realities of student life and congregational and community ministry afforded by campus life. As realization of these losses crashes in upon them, it is natural for faculty members to resist calls for change and to rationalize perpetuation of the status quo.

Seminary administrators must recognize the losses sustained by faculty members as the seminary transitions to transformational teaching and learning.[11] Some faculty members will take longer than others to let go of the past. Resistance, even anger, should not be surprising. Rather than meeting resistance with debate or demands, losses should be acknowledged openly and sympathetically. That which was accomplished in the past can be celebrated, even as the prospect of a new fruitfulness is embraced. All losses, ultimately, must be weighed against the futility of teaching which quickly dissipates and which yields ministries that contribute to immaturity and impotence in the church. Yes, the losses are real, but the future of ministry education that transforms is abundantly more rewarding.

Communicate, Communicate, Communicate

Grief over losses, the challenge of learning new ways to perceive and embody one's role as seminary teacher, learning new ways to teach, and the sheer work of redesigning courses make it easy to lose sight of the goal. Like the proverbial mason, laying block for a medieval cathedral, faculty members may conceive their task as revising syllabi or designing new lesson plans. They need to be reminded often that their task, instead, is developing spiritually transformed

---

10. Bridges, 24.

11. Bridges's chapter on "How to Get People to Let Go" (23–38) is very helpful.

leaders whose ministries will result in transformed believers, congregations, and communities.

From the moment the seminary acknowledges its contribution to the immaturity and impotence of the church and determines to embrace a new vision of its ministry for the sake of the church, the seminary president, principal, or rector must hold that vision before the faculty, the seminary's alumni, and its constituent church. Every communication should remind others why the seminary has set out upon this transitional journey and where it is headed. The vision of a spiritually dynamic church engaged in making disciples and in advocating for biblical values in community, marketplace, and government is energizing. Members of the faculty and the constituent church need to be reminded of this vision over and over.

Faculty members also need to be reminded that transformational teaching and learning is possible and is critical to that vision. Only as faculty members embrace teaching for obedience to God's truth as a means of shaping character, skills, and knowledge will students' lives be transformed. That transformation is essential to transformation of the church.

Collectively Pursue Transformation as Alignment with the Missio Dei

Transformed lives and ministries are important because this is God's intention and desire for his church. God does not intend his people to live in defeat. He desires to demonstrate his power and his glory through his people. Christians are "a chosen race, a royal priesthood, a holy nation, a people for [God's] own possession, that [they] may proclaim the excellencies of him who called [them] out of darkness into his marvelous light" (1 Pet 2:9). By submitting fully to God's will, by appropriating his grace for a life of obedience and fruitfulness, faculty members model the transformed life which is the goal of their teaching. As they teach for transformation of life and ministry, they also equip students to see God's desire fulfilled through their ministries. Spiritually vital and biblically faithful churches bring glory to God. They also confront evil and injustice and call their communities and nations to submit to God's truth.

Ministry education that transforms is also critically important because only a transformed church will fulfill the Great Commission. It is the church's task to make disciples in all the world, baptizing them into local communities of believers, and teaching them to obey all that Christ commanded (Matt 28:19–20). God takes no pleasure in those who are Christian in name only, with worldviews, values, and priorities that are unchanged from their pre-Christian past. God desires children – from every culture and nation – who are like him, who love him, and with whom he can relate intimately.

The Vision of a Transformed Church

Change may seem threatening and will be challenging but it is possible. Transformational perspectives and methods can be learned. Faculty members can teach for transformation of life and ministry. The seminary can become an engine for vitalization of the church and expansion of Christ's kingdom. Hundreds of faculty members from seminaries and theological colleges across the Majority World already have seen this potential and are exhibiting dynamic commitment and skill to teach for life and ministry transformation.[12] As we "sell the problem" of the seminary's responsibility for the spiritual impotence of the church, we also must assure the church and its seminaries that transformational teaching and learning is a realistic goal – that dramatic change really is possible.

Seminary graduates can model and mentor believers toward transformed lives marked by worldviews, values, and priorities aligned with God's own. They can lead congregations to experience the transformation they themselves know as they love God, daily encounter him in intimacy, and walk in obedience to his Word. They can see their congregations choose simple lifestyles and stewardship of all God's blessings. Their churches and parachurch ministries can be magnets, drawing non-Christians to the Savior and propelling apostolic missionaries into ministries among the world's least reached.

Communities in which seminary graduates serve also can be impacted by God's transformation of his church. As the church models relational wholeness and love for its community, the watching world will respond in one of two ways. Some will be more adamant in their rejection and will bring increasing pressure against the church. Others, however, will be drawn to the beauty of the church's life and witness. Those engaged in evil and oppression of the vulnerable will be challenged to turn to Christ for forgiveness and deliverance from their sinful

---

12. See appendix A.

ways. Local and national leaders will be confronted, respectfully and lovingly, with God's expectation that they will pursue peace and justice for all.

What a beautiful vision of a society and culture marked by the faith and witness of God's people, of churches and parachurch ministries led by men and women whose lives are aligned with God's values and priorities, and of seminaries where students' lives are transformed by obedience to the truth of God's revelation and by the exemplary lives of their teachers! This is the vision that motivates the drive toward transformational theological education. We invite you to join us in this vision and on this journey.

Appendices

Appendix A

A Brief History of GATE

The origins of Global Associates for Transformational Education (GATE) date back to the mid-1990s when Columbia Biblical Seminary and School of Missions offered a master's degree in International Theological Education. Although the degree program attracted a few students, it quickly became evident that those pursuing studies and research in international theological education typically held a master's degree; what was needed were doctoral qualifications. Furthermore, there were clear advantages to offering the program in conjunction with a public university, both for access to resources and for recognition by foreign governments of the degree earned.

Initial Impediments

For three years, Robert Ferris, the seminary's Director of Doctoral Studies, met with Department of Higher Education deans and program directors from nearby University of South Carolina's College of Education. In the course of dialogue, a rationale was presented that a cadre of international students would enrich the doctoral experience of all students pursuing the university's PhD in Higher Education. A program was designed and approved by the faculties of the seminary and the university's Department of Higher Education that provided for elective requirements in the university's PhD in Higher Education Administration to be satisfied by courses in international theological education taught at the seminary. The collaborative degree program, however, was never realized. The university accepted a very limited annual intake of doctoral students in Higher Education and priority was assigned to in-State applicants.

As the vision of a collaborative PhD in international theological education began to unravel, Ferris and Columbia International University Provost Ralph Enlow considered launching a doctoral program in international theological education. Enlow convened a consultation at the Awana Ministries Center in Streamwood, Illinois, 7–9 September 2000, to seek advice. Participants at the consultation included Enlow and Ferris, James Pleuddemann of SIM International, Duane Elmer and Linda Cannell of Trinity Evangelical Divinity School, and John Lillis of Bethel Seminary, San Diego.

The proposal that initially emerged from this 2000 consultation envisioned a PhD or EdD program with a "virtual faculty" and program elements offered through workshops and seminars, as well as more traditional courses. Ferris was charged with drafting a "working paper" to flesh out the concept.

While this proposal seemed to address some impediments to a program of doctoral studies in international theological education, it did not address others. Aspects of university education – such as need for program recognition, a culture of academic elitism, bias toward research and accumulation of information versus learning in context, demands of accrediting agencies – tend to diverge from the ministry training needs of the global church. When even this proposal seemed financially out of reach due to the relatively high cost of scholarship assistance required by qualified students, a decision was taken to explore addressing the recognized need through a nonformal education project.

Conversation, Collaboration, and Concept Development

Enlow, Ferris, Elmer, and Lillis dialogued periodically about the need for a nonformal education project but all were fully engaged at their respective institutions and little progress was realized. During this time, Lillis collected calls from the Majority World for alternative approaches to ministry preparation. Ferris also drafted a proposal for "Enhancing Global Theological Education" that was circulated among this project group.

In the fall of 2002, Elmer was invited to lead a workshop track at the European Leadership Forum, to be held in Sopron, Hungary, in May 2003. Elmer proposed exploring the need for an alternative model of ministry preparation with participants at the forum and invited Enlow, Ferris, and

Lillis to collaborate with him in developing and delivering the workshop track sessions. Ferris had a schedule conflict with the May dates, but the other three attended the forum and facilitated both the track workshops and an informal group discussion of perceived needs and proposed solutions.

The informal discussion session was attended by about thirty East European pastors and seminary leaders. The consensus among the East Europeans was that current theological education was, in many cases, failing to equip pastors to meet the needs of the church, to address the problems of culture, and to speak relevantly to the emerging generation. The sentiments of many present in the meeting were aptly summarized by Nik Nedelchev, then President of Bulgarian Evangelical Theological Institute and subsequently President of the European Evangelical Alliance. Nedelchev said, "We imported the best theological education models from the West and they are not doing the job of training our pastors."

The team returned from the forum in Sopron highly motivated to address the needs that had been expressed. Elmer obtained a grant to underwrite the cost of workshops in Kiev, Ukraine, and Prague, Czech Republic. Planning meetings were held and responsibilities assigned. The name "Global Associates for Transformational Education" was adopted, guiding principles were framed, and a three-year curriculum was envisioned. Three annual workshops would be offered: Year 1 – "Biblical and Theoretical Foundations for Transformational Education"; Year 2 – "Methods of Teaching for Transformation"; and Year 3 – "Leadership for Transformative Learning." The team reached a strong collective conviction that, in order to overcome institutional inertia and increase the likelihood of deep and enduring institutional change, participating schools would be encouraged to bring their entire faculty and sessions would be structured to facilitate interaction among all participants. All four Associates committed to participate in the initial workshops in Kiev and Prague in June 2004.

Initiating the Workshop Cycle

Because of mixed messages from the Ukrainian Embassy in Chicago, Elmer and Enlow did not obtain visas for the Ukraine. Elmer was turned back after arriving in Kiev and Enlow was not allowed to board his connecting flight in London. Ferris and Lillis learned, after arriving in Kiev, that they would facilitate the initial workshop without the assistance of their colleagues. Fortunately, the team had exchanged session plans; Ferris facilitated sessions he had prepared and those originally assigned to Elmer; Lillis facilitated sessions he had prepared and those assigned to Enlow. The workshop was held at Ukrainian Evangelical Theological Seminary, with forty faculty members from twelve seminaries attending. That workshop sessions were translated into Russian was a challenge but the workshop was well received.

Dr Sergiy Sannikov, Director of Euro-Asian Accrediting Association (EAAA), was present at the Kiev workshop. He immediately recognized the value of the GATE workshop and adopted GATE as a professional development opportunity that he promoted among EAAA member schools until his 2009 retirement as EAAA's Director.

The full GATE team was present for the workshop in Prague, held at the International Baptist Theological Seminary. Among the forty-three participants in that workshop was Nik Nedelchev, from Bulgarian Evangelical Theological Institute. By the conclusion of the workshop, Nedelchev implored the GATE team to schedule workshops in Bulgaria. As a result, Ferris and Elmer traveled to Sofia in October, 2004, where they facilitated GATE's third workshop for about twenty-eight faculty members. Although Elmer and Ferris were assured that all faculty members spoke English, they quickly recognized that translation into Bulgarian was needed in order for participants to fully grasp the meaning and implications of concepts and principles presented. In its first year, therefore, GATE held a Year 1 workshop in three nations of the former Soviet Union, touched 111 Bible college and seminary faculty members, and established a partnership with EAAA.

In 2005, Year 2 workshops were held in the locations established the previous year and a new sequence of workshops was launched in Moscow. Moscow proved to be an expensive venue, however, so the rest of the workshops in that cycle were relocated to Odessa, Ukraine. The team also recognized that the three-year curriculum initially envisioned must be extended with the addition of a Year 4 workshop on "Developing Curricula for Transformational Education."

A Global Network through Regional Partnerships

As word about GATE workshops spread, the team received an increasing number of requests to provide workshops in other regions. Dieumème Noelliste, of Caribbean Evangelical Theological Association, was particularly insistent that GATE should provide workshops in the Caribbean region but the team found its capacity limited by time and funding.

In 2008, with completion of the initial four-year sequence of workshops in Eastern Europe, the GATE team was ready to expand its area of service. Ferris and Lillis had contacts in Asia which led to offering the GATE workshops in the Philippines; Elmer and Ferris also had contacts with leaders of the Association for Christian Theological Education in Africa (ACTEA)[1] which led to offering the workshops in Kenya and Ethiopia, beginning in 2008. In the Philippines, workshops were scheduled in Manila and Davao, and in East Africa, workshops were scheduled in Nairobi, Kenya, and at Lake Langano, Ethiopia. From the outset, Asia Graduate School of Theology (a program of Asia Theological Association) co-sponsored GATE workshops in the Philippines and ACTEA co-sponsored GATE workshops in East Africa. The leadership of Theresa Lua, of AGST, and Stephanie Black and Philippe Emedi, of ACTEA, was crucial to the success of workshops in their regions. In 2010, Elmer advised the other members of the GATE team that he wished to pursue other opportunities and discontinued active participation in the project.

Throughout the first decade of its ministry the GATE team continued to develop and revise its workshop curriculum. Each workshop was evaluated by participants and debriefed by the GATE team. Lessons learned were documented and curricula were refined.

In 2010, the Overseas Council (OC)[2] requested GATE to offer jointly sponsored workshops in India and in Togo, West Africa, but specified that the workshops should be offered in a two-year, rather than four-year, sequence. The GATE team agreed to offer the workshops as requested on a trial basis. The Year 1 and Year 2 workshop sessions were merged into a five-day workshop schedule and workshops were held in Bangalore, India, and in Lomé, Togo, in 2011. In 2012, the Year 3 and Year 4 workshop sessions were offered in the

---

1. Then, the Accrediting Council for Theological Education in Africa.
2. Then, the Overseas Council International (OCI).

same venues. While the workshops were well received, the GATE team decided that the original commitment to a four-year workshop cycle was wise. The larger number of interventions with each faculty enhances the probability of institutional change and affords three opportunities (versus only one) to debrief faculty members on implementation of lessons learned and to provide counsel on overcoming barriers encountered.

Staff members of OC and members of the GATE team periodically interacted both informally and formally even before the formation of GATE. When Ferris was invited to meet with OC's International Ministries staff in 2011, he invited staff members to attend a GATE workshop as observers. In April 2012, Josué Fernández, OC Regional Director for Latin America and the Caribbean, and Riad Kassis, then OC Regional Director for Europe and the Middle East, observed Year 4 workshops in the Philippines. The men were excited by the workshops observed and Fernández insisted that GATE should launch workshops in Latin America and the Caribbean the following year.

In 2014, Taras Dyatlik, OC Regional Director for Eastern Europe and Director of EAAA, observed a GATE Year 1 Workshop in Nairobi. Without prior personal experience in a GATE workshop, Dyatlik arrived in Nairobi skeptical of the value of the GATE project and its appropriateness in EAAA's context. By the second day of the workshop, however, he recognized that the workshop offered, in his words, "exactly the training needed by faculties in the EAAA region." Unfortunately, political unrest and Russian military action in the Ukraine in 2014 made it impossible to launch a new cycle of GATE workshops in the Ukraine or Russia at that time.

A Global Team of Training Associates

From the outset, the GATE team recognized that transformational education advocacy and training resources must be situated in the regions of the schools and churches it is designed to serve and that the GATE team should include Associates from every global region. In March 2012, the GATE team held a "Training the Trainers" workshop in Orlando, Florida, to which three well-qualified candidates were invited. John Jusu, a Sierra Leonean with a PhD in Educational Ministries from Trinity Evangelical Divinity School, had worked with GATE Associates in facilitating workshops in Nairobi, Kenya, Lake

Langano, Ethiopia, and Odessa, Ukraine. Joanna Feliciano Soberano, a Filipina who also holds a PhD in Educational Ministries from Trinity Evangelical Divinity School, had worked with GATE Associates in facilitating workshops in both Manila and Davao, Philippines. Gary Griffith, an American who served for fourteen years in Bulgaria and holds a PhD in New Testament from the Durham University, had participated in GATE workshops while serving on the faculty of Bulgaria Evangelical Institute of Theology. "Training the Trainers" sessions were designed to acquaint participants with GATE's mission, core values, and educational philosophy. At the end of the workshop, the GATE team was expanded from three to six Associates.

The next step was taken in 2013, when GATE workshops were launched in Latin America. Josué Fernández, of Overseas Council, identified twelve theological educators from across Latin America and the Caribbean to be trained as GATE Associates. Because these educators had not personally experienced a GATE workshop, a two-week training workshop was scheduled in Quito, Ecuador. During the first week, the GATE team facilitated a Year 1– Year 2 workshop for three Ecuadorian seminaries while the trainees observed the workshop sessions. During the second week, the GATE team reviewed the curricula for the Year 3 and Year 4 workshops while introducing the trainees to GATE's core values and philosophy of education. The trainees were divided into three teams and assigned to facilitate a Year 1 workshop within the next twelve months, coached by a GATE Associate. One team was assigned to facilitate a workshop in the Caribbean, another in Mexico, and the third in Brazil. The workshop cycles launched in these sites in 2014 were completed in 2017, with nine of the original twelve trainees, plus one trainee who joined the team later, completing the training and appointed as GATE Associates.

When "Training the Trainer" cycles were launched in the Philippines and East Africa in 2014, all trainees had already completed GATE's four-year curriculum as workshop participants. The training curriculum was adapted, furthermore, to permit trainees to observe workshops one year at a time. Thus, in 2014, GATE Associates launched a new cycle of workshops in Nairobi and in Manila, with the trainees as observers. Throughout the workshops, Associates debriefed sessions with the trainees and, following the workshop, trainees were provided with additional training in GATE's values and educational philosophy, as well as in educational theory that supported the session just observed. Then, during the following year, trainees were assigned to teams and required to facilitate a workshop like the one observed, coached by a GATE Associate. This training model has proven more satisfactory than the one used in Latin America and the Caribbean. It was agreed that, in the future, trainees should have experienced the GATE workshops as faculty participants before entering the Training the Trainers program.

A Global Enterprise Increasing in Global Impact

In 2018, when all trainees have completed the present Training the Trainers cycle, GATE's roster is expected to comprise thirty-two Associates – eleven women and twenty-one men – from thirteen nations of Asia, Africa, Latin America, North America, and the Caribbean. Through 2017, GATE has conducted seventy-five workshops[3] in twenty-three venues with an enrollment of 2,449 faculty participants, including at least 779 unduplicated faculty members[4] from 110 Bible colleges and seminaries in twenty-four nations. Funding to underwrite GATE's ministry has been provided by friends, churches, and partner foundations in the United States. For all this, we give God glory.

---

3. An additional thirteen workshops are scheduled to complete the current training cycles in 2018.

4. This represents the total participants in Year 1 workshops; since other faculty members join the workshops in Year 2 or following, the actual unduplicated number of participants is higher.

Appendix B

GATE's Philosophy of Teaching and Learning

As the GATE team faced the troubling reality of superficial Christianity in the global church, its response was guided by several observations and commitments.

Commitment to Effect Organizational Change

In contrast to incumbent models of education that focus on transfer of information, educational theory and research confirm the Hebraic understanding that learning is incomplete until it has been enacted. In order to allow greater opportunity for application of learning, the team provides new information and skill training in small units. Rather than scheduling five- or ten-day workshops, each workshop is planned as a three-day event with successive workshops scheduled annually over a four-year cycle. During each workshop, faculties plan implementation of the information and skills gained. Furthermore, at the beginning of each successive workshop, participants are invited to report on application of learning gained the previous year. Difficulties reported afford opportunity for collective reflection by participants and facilitators on strategies to avoid and to overcome those specific barriers.

Research on organizational change also indicates the probability of change increases when a majority of community members understand and embrace an innovation and its means of implementation. Therefore, the GATE team limits the number of participating schools with the aim of engaging a majority of faculty members, if not the entire faculty, of each participating institution. To provide incentive for majority faculty participation, registration is charged on an institutional basis; the cost is the same whether two faculty members or the entire faculty attends. A 40 percent discount is given, however, to any institution that registers a substantial majority of its faculty. A further 20 percent discount is given to schools when the president, principal, vice chancellor, or rector attends. The effect has been to ensure that for most participating institutions a majority of faculty members and administrative leaders are familiar with the perspectives and methodologies of transformational education.

Theological and Hermeneutical Commitments

True life transformation is a work of God; teachers can challenge learners to think critically about assumptions and values but only God can extend grace needed to change a person's heart. Learners must choose to adopt new ways but grace is needed to overcome egocentric bias and established patterns in order to choose biblically and missionally effective ways of thinking, acting, relating, and teaching.

The primary instruments used by the Holy Spirit to effect transformational change are the Holy Scriptures and the example of teachers and leaders who model alternative perspectives, strategies, and relationships. The Scriptures provide the essential content for life transformation and therefore must be taught with fidelity to authorial intent as indicated by linguistic and historical attention to both the immediate and canonical contexts.

The life of the leader – in schooling contexts, the faculty and its administration – is equally critical since it constitutes the implicit curriculum studied and learned by others. If truths taught are not validated in practice, they are likely to be disregarded. For this reason, the team designs GATE workshops to demonstrate the biblical and educational values and the relational and instructional methods that are taught. These values, as well as the undergirding theological and educational principles, constitute a critical aspect of GATE's training for new Associates.

The Nature of Truth

While acknowledging that each individual constructs her or his understanding of truth, the GATE team rejects the unbiblical assertion that all truth is personal and, therefore, relative. Specifically, in the areas of God's revelation and the physical world, truth claims can be tested and untruth falsified, exposed, and rejected. Following God's revealed tests of a prophet (Deut 13:1–5; 18:20–22), the team examines truth claims for consistency with prior revelation (i.e. with the theological and moral teachings of the Scriptures) and for consistency with the world of realities, empirically observed.

Contextual Appropriateness

The GATE team's commitment to objective truth does not discount the importance of contextual realities. The team seeks to understand the contexts of the faculties that participate in GATE workshops, including those of students and constituent churches. As the team shares biblical and educational principles, the question frequently is asked, "How does this work in your context?"

Commitment to contextualization is a core GATE value. The original team of four has been intentional in developing a culturally diverse team of thirty-two women and men from Asia, Africa, Latin America, and the Caribbean, as well as North America. Because these embedded advocates of transformative change understand the cultural and ecclesial contexts in which they work, they can be more effective in adapting the values, perspectives, and methods of transformational education to the schools and churches of their respective regions.

A View of the Learner

Learners are persons who bear the image of God and therefore have great value. Relationships that degrade or manipulate learners are inherently inappropriate in the learning environment. In GATE workshops, the team models respect for learners and for one another. Our team approach affords multiple opportunities to affirm one another and to reinforce contributions from workshop participants. When observations or opinions are offered that reflect misunderstandings or are unhelpful, they are respectfully challenged. Because the workshop environment is dialogical, this occurs naturally.

Learners have untapped capacity to learn and to change. We see many evidences that GATE workshop participants want to honor God in their teaching and want to see transformative change in their learners. This affords encouragement to challenge learners to reassess their educational assumptions and practices in the light of biblical principles and best educational practices. When biblical truth and the perspectives and methods of transformational education are appropriately modeled and taught, we see learners embrace and implement strategies that foster transformational change.

The Purpose of Education

Education should provide an environment rich in biblical truth, appropriately taught and modeled, that the Holy Spirit can use to transform the lives of learners. The goal of education should be to equip learners with information, strategies, and perspectives appropriate to their calling within their community and culture.

Because the term is used variously in educational literature, we find it necessary to define "Transformational Education." As used by the GATE team, "Transformational Education" occurs when an institution and a teacher create an environment – through personal modeling, through curricular and course design, and through in-class and out-of-class interaction – that encourages learners to integrate God's truth into their fundamental perspectives, core values, relational patterns, and habits of life, thereby opening themselves to God's transforming power. Institutions and teachers that create such environments can be described as engaged in transformational education. When learners are transformed by God's grace, the effect extends to every aspect of life and is lived out in community.

The Role of the Teacher

God holds accountable those who teach (Jas 3:1) and, therefore, teachers are obligated to be subject-matter experts in their discipline fields. The calling of the teacher, however, is not primarily to transfer information but to employ information shared toward the goal of life transformation. In this regard, it is critical, as previously noted, that the teacher should embody, and thus model for learners, application of the truths taught.

In the classroom, on campus, and in the community, we share information, nurture curiosity, and develop research skills, we model and encourage reflection on undergirding principles and cognitive structures, we teach and practice relational and ministry skills, and we identify, explore, challenge (as appropriate), and thus shape students' perspectives regarding the teaching–learning process, the Christian life, the church's ministry, and their personal calling.

The teachers also need to know their learners – their context of present or envisioned ministry, their individual and family contexts, their prior educational histories, and their personal fears, challenges, joys, callings, and aspirations. Learning is a social event but teaching always is personal and relational. Only when we, as teachers, know our learners can we effectively shape the learning context for the Holy Spirit's transformational work. Thus, the teacher teaches for holistic understanding and application of truth in the context of the learner.

Appendix C

GATE's Workshop Curriculum[1]

GATE offers a series of four annual workshops. We refer to them as workshops because the room in which we meet becomes a "shop" in which, together, we work to understand the implications of our theological commitments for the way we plan educational programs and the ways we teach. As a GATE team, we bring to the workshops a robust integration of biblical theology, grounded theory, and educational research in human cognition, the psychology of learning, and organizational change. Our methodology in the workshops is to set a context in which faculties can interact with theory, theology, and their cultural and institutional realities in ways that facilitate and encourage institutional change.

Theological and Philosophical Foundations for Transformational Education / Year 1

This workshop engages the participants in a discovery process to determine how factors such as the characteristics of entering students, the nature of the church, and the realities of their own cultures impact the designs and outcomes of educational experiences. Special emphasis is given to introducing relevant biblical/theological categories as well as modeling established educational practices. Faculties set institutional and individual goals for the year ahead.

---

1. From https://www.gateglobal.org/curriculum.html.

Teaching Methods for Transformational Education / Year 2

In this workshop participants explore classroom methodology that leads to life transformation rather than the mere processing of information. Participants discover that designing educational experiences that promote transformational learning involves more than just organizing and delivering content. Special attention is given to the wide variety of methods used by Jesus as well as the purposes he had for using different approaches. In this and each succeeding workshop, faculties report on how well they achieved their goals from the previous year and set institutional and individual goals for the year ahead.

Leadership That Transforms Education / Year 3

This workshop considers how administrative practices such as leadership styles, decision-making, personnel management, and conflict resolution impact the learning of students in a school. Participants examine the values that inform these practices and what students are learning through this hidden or implicit curriculum of the school. Biblical metaphors for leadership and leadership development are discussed with a view to making appropriate changes in practice for given situations.

Developing Curriculum for Transformational Education / Year 4

The final workshop addresses the school's curriculum and how it should be shaped based upon the ministry context that its graduates will encounter. Participants consider how the state of the local church, the local culture, as well as biblical and cultural requirements for church leaders impact the school's curriculum design. A key component of this workshop is the creation of a ministry profile describing the skills and character traits necessary for ministry in the local context. The workshop is intended to produce significant short-term and long-term institutional adjustments and individual course refinements for those participating.

Appendix D

Year 1 Workshop Schedule Template

Time*	Day 1	Day 2	Day 3	Day 4
8:00–8:30		Breakfast	Breakfast	Breakfast
8:45–9:15		Morning Devotions	Morning Devotions	Morning Devotions
9:15–10:30		01: Metaphors for Teaching and Learning	03: Incoming Students & Future Challenges	05: The Learning Cycle
10:30–11:00		Morning Break	Morning Break	Morning Break
11:00–12:30		Metaphors for Teaching and Learning – cont.	Incoming Students & Future Challenges – cont.	Closing Session: Expectations Gift Books Certificates Workshop Evaluation
12:30–14:00	GATE Team Lunch	Lunch and Siesta	Lunch and Siesta	Lunch and Siesta

14:00–15:30	Arrival and Registration	02: Qualities of Graduates, Biblical Leaders	04: Paradigm Shift: Teaching to Learning	Faculty Participants' Departure
15:30–16:00		Afternoon Break	Afternoon Break	Afternoon Break
16:00–17:30		Qualities of Graduates, Biblical Leaders – cont.	Paradigm Shift: Teaching to Learning – cont.	GATE Team Debrief
18:00–18:45	Dinner	Dinner	Dinner	Dinner
19:00–21:00	Venue Welcome GATE Welcome Workshop Theme Expectations Introductions	Fellowship Free Time	Fellowship‡ Free Time	GATE Team Departure

* Note: The schedule should be adjusted to reflect the normal meal schedule at the workshop venue. Each extended session should be about three hours in two ninety-minute segments.

‡ If additional time is desired for Session 05: "The Learning Cycle," the evening session on Day 3 may be used.

Appendix E

Further Reading

Piaget

Jardine, David William. *Piaget and Education Primer*. New York: Peter Lang, 2006.
Labinowicz, Ed. *The Piaget Primer: Thinking, Learning, Teaching*. Menlo Park, CA: Addison-Wesley, 1980.

Freire

Freire, Paulo. *Education for Critical Consciousness*. 1st American ed. New York: Seabury, 1973.
———. *Pedagogy of the Oppressed*. 13th anniversary ed. New York: Continuum, 2000.
Gadotti, Moacir. *Reading Paulo Freire: His Life and Work*. Albany, NY: State University of New York Press, 1994.

Vella

Vella, Jane. *Learning to Listen, Learning to Teach: The Power of Dialogue in Educating Adults*. Rev. ed. San Francisco: Jossey-Bass, 2002.
———. *On Teaching and Learning*. San Francisco: Jossey-Bass, 2008.
———. *Taking Learning to Task*. San Francisco: Jossey-Bass, 2001.

Bloom

Anderson, Lorin W., and David R. Krathwohl, eds. *A Taxonomy for Learning, Teaching, and Assessing: A Revision of Bloom's Taxonomy of Educational Objectives.* Abridged ed. New York: Pearson, 2001.

Brain-Imaging Technology

Johnson, Sandra, and Kathleen Taylor. *The Neuroscience of Adult Learning.* New Directions for Adult and Continuing Education 110. San Francisco: Jossey-Bass, 2006.

Zull, James E. *Art of Changing the Brain.* Dulles, VA: Stylus, 2011.

———. *From Brain to Mind: Using Neuroscience to Guide Change in Education.* Sterling, VA: Stylus, 2011.

Kolb

Kolb, D. A. *Experiential Learning.* Englewood Cliffs, NJ: Prentice Hall, 1984.

Mezirow

Cranton, Patricia. *Understanding and Promoting Transformative Learning: A Guide for Educators of Adults.* San Francisco: Jossey-Bass, 1994.

Mezirow, Jack. *Fostering Critical Reflection in Adulthood: A Guide to Transformative and Emancipatory Learning.* San Francisco: Jossey-Bass, 1990.

———. *Transformative Dimensions of Adult Learning.* San Francisco: Jossey-Bass, 1991.

Bibliography

Anderson, Keith R., and Randy D. Reese. *Spiritual Mentoring: A Guide for Seeking and Giving Direction*. Downers Grove, IL: InterVarsity, 1999.

Anderson, Lorin W., and David R. Krathwohl, eds. *A Taxonomy for Learning, Teaching, and Assessing: A Revision of Bloom's Taxonomy of Educational Objectives*. New York: Pearson Education, 2000.

Awbrey, Susan M. "General Education Reform as Organizational Change: Integrating Cultural and Structural Change." *Journal of General Education* 54, no. 1 (2005): 5.

Barclay, William. *Educational Ideals in the Ancient World*. Grand Rapids: Baker, 1959.

Bloom, Benjamin S., Max D. Engelhart, Edward J. Furst, Walker H. Hill, and David R. Krathwohl. *Taxonomy of Educational Objectives: Handbook 1, The Cognitive Domain*. New York: Longman, 1956.

Bridges, William. *Managing Transitions*. Cambridge, MA: Da Capo Press, 1991.

Brookfield, Stephen D. *The Skillful Teacher*. 2nd ed. San Francisco: Jossey-Bass, 2006.

Center for Global Christianity. "Christianity in Its Global Context: 1970–2020: Society, Religion, and Mission." Gordon-Conwell Theological Seminary, June 2013. Accessed 15 March 2017. http://www.gordonconwell.edu/ockenga/research/documents/ChristianityinitsGlobalContext.pdf.

Cranton, Patricia. "Self-Directed and Transformational Instructional Development." *Journal of Higher Education* 65, no. 6 (1994): 726–744.

——— "Teaching for Transformation." *New Directions for Adult and Continuing Education* 2002, no. 93 (2002): 63–72.

———. *Understanding and Promoting Transformative Learning: A Guide for Educators of Adults*. San Francisco: Jossey-Bass, 2006.

Crouch, Andy. *Playing God: Redeeming the Gift of Power*. Downers Grove, IL: InterVarsity, 2013.

El-Khawas, Elaine. *Accreditation in the USA: Origins, Developments, and Future Prospects*. Paris: International Institute for Educational Planning, UNESCO, 2001. Accessed 27 July 2017. http://unesdoc.unesco.org/images/0012/001292/ 129295e.pdf.

Elmer, Duane. *Cross-Cultural Conflict: Building Relationships for Effective Ministry*. Downers Grove, IL: InterVarsity, 1993.

Enlow, Ralph E. *The Leader's Palette*. Bloomington, IN: Westbow, 2013.

Epstein, M. J., and K. Yuthas. *Measuring and Improving Social Impacts*. San Francisco: Barrett-Koehler, 2014.

Ewell, Peter T. "An Emerging Scholarship: A Brief History of Assessment." National Center for Higher Education Management Systems (NCHEMS). Accessed 29 July 2017. https://westmoreland.edu/media/124908/ie-assessment-info-6-a_brief_history_of_assessment.pdf.

Ferris, Robert W., ed. *Establishing Ministry Training: A Manual for Programme Developers*. Pasadena, CA: William Carey Library, 1995.

Foster, Richard. *Celebration of Discipline: The Path to Spiritual Growth*. 3rd ed. New York: HarperCollins, 1998.

Freire, Paulo. *Pedagogy of the Oppressed*. New York: Seabury, 1970.

Hiebert, Paul G. *Transforming Worldviews: An Anthropological Understanding of How People Change*. Grand Rapids: Baker Academic, 2008.

Horne, Herman. *Jesus the Teacher*. Grand Rapids: Kregel, 1998.

Jackson, Philip. *Life in Classrooms*. New York: Holt, Rinehart and Winston, 1968.

Johnson, D. W., R. T. Johnson, and K. A. Smith. *Active Learning: Cooperation in the College Classroom*. Edina, MN: Interaction Book Company, 2006.

Kinsler, F. Ross. "Bases for Change in Theological Education." In *The Extension Movement in Theological Education*, rev. ed., 3–24. Pasadena, CA: William Carey Library, 1978, 1981.

Kolb, D. A. *Experiential Learning*. Englewood Cliffs, NJ: Prentice Hall, 1984.

Kotter, John. *The Heart of Change*. Boston: Harvard Business School, 2002.

———. *Leading Change*. Boston: Harvard Business School, 1996.

Krathwohl, David R. "A Revision of Bloom's Taxonomy: An Overview." *Theory Into Practice* 41, no. 4 (Autumn 2002): 212–218.

Krathwohl, David R., Benjamin S. Bloom, and Bertram B. Masia. *Taxonomy of Educational Objectives: Handbook 2, The Affective Domain*. New York: Longman, 1957.

Lipka, Michael, and Conrad Hackett. "Why Muslims Are the World's Fastest Growing Religious Group." Pew Research, 6 April 2017. Accessed 21 September 2017. http://www.pewresearch.org/fact-tank/2017/04/06/why-muslims-are-the-worlds-fastest-growing-religious-group/.

Lyall, Leslie T. *A Passion for the Impossible: The Continuing Story of the Mission Hudson Taylor Began*. London: OMF, 1965.

Mezirow, Jack. *Education for Perspective Transformation: Women's Re-Entry Programs in Community Colleges*. New York: Center for Adult Education, Teachers College, Columbia University, 1978.

————. *Fostering Critical Reflection in Adulthood: A Guide to Transformative and Emancipatory Learning*. San Francisco: Jossey-Bass, 1990.

————. "Transformative Learning: Theory to Practice." *New Directions for Adult and Continuing Education* 1997, no. 74 (1997): 5–12.

Mulholland, M. Robert, Jr. *Invitation to a Journey: A Road Map for Spiritual Formation*. Downers Grove, IL: InterVarsity, 1993.

Palmer, Parker. *The Courage to Teach: Exploring the Inner Landscape of a Teacher's Life*. San Francisco: Jossey-Bass, 1998.

Peterson, Eugene. *Eat This Book: A Conversation in the Art of Spiritual Reading*. Grand Rapids: Eerdmans, 2006.

Rice, Brian K. *The Exercises, Volume One: Conversations*. York, PA: Leadership ConneXtions International, 2012.

Skinner, B. F. *Science and Human Behavior*. New York: Free Press, 1953.

Taylor, Edward W. "Analyzing Research on Transformational Learning Theory." In Jack Mezirow and Associates, *Learning as Transformation: Critical Perspectives on a Theory in Progress*, 1st ed., 285–328 (San Francisco: Jossey-Bass, 2000).

Tyler, Ralph W. *Basic Principles of Curriculum and Instruction*. Chicago: University of Chicago Press, 1949.

Vella, Jane. *Learning to Listen, Learning to Teach*. Rev. ed. San Francisco: Jossey-Bass, 2002.

————. *On Teaching and Learning*. San Francisco: Jossey-Bass, 2008.

————. *Taking Learning to Task*. San Francisco: Jossey-Bass, 2001.

Weimer, Maryellen. *Learner-Centered Teaching*. San Francisco: Jossey-Bass, 2002.

Willard, Dallas. *The Divine Conspiracy: Rediscovering Our Hidden Life in God*. Downers Grove, IL: InterVarsity, 1998.

————. *Hearing God: Developing a Conversational Relationship with God*. Downers Grove, IL: InterVarsity, 2012.

————. *The Spirit of the Disciplines: Understanding How God Changes Lives*. Downers Grove, IL: InterVarsity, 1999.

Zuck, Roy B. *Teaching as Jesus Taught*. Grand Rapids: Baker, 1995.

Zull, James E. *The Art of Changing the Brain: Enriching the Practice of Teaching by Exploring the Biology of Learning*. Sterling, VA: Stylus, 2002.

ICETE International Council for Evangelical Theological Education

strengthening evangelical theological education through international cooperation

ICETE is a global community, sponsored by nine regional networks of theological schools, to enable international interaction and collaboration among all those engaged in strengthening and developing evangelical theological education and Christian leadership development worldwide.

The purpose of ICETE is:

1. To promote the enhancement of evangelical theological education worldwide.
2. To serve as a forum for interaction, partnership and collaboration among those involved in evangelical theological education and leadership development, for mutual assistance, stimulation and enrichment.
3. To provide networking and support services for regional associations of evangelical theological schools worldwide.
4. To facilitate among these bodies the advancement of their services to evangelical theological education within their regions.

Sponsoring associations include:

Africa: Association for Christian Theological Education in Africa (ACTEA)

Asia: Asia Theological Association (ATA)

Caribbean: Caribbean Evangelical Theological Association (CETA)

Europe: European Evangelical Accrediting Association (EEAA)

Euro-Asia: Euro-Asian Accrediting Association (E-AAA)

Latin America: Association for Evangelical Theological Education in Latin America (AETAL)

Middle East and North Africa: Middle East Association for Theological Education (MEATE)

North America: Association for Biblical Higher Education (ABHE)

South Pacific: South Pacific Association of Evangelical Colleges (SPAEC)

www.icete-edu.org

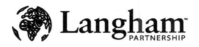

Langham Literature and its imprints are a ministry of Langham Partnership.

Langham Partnership is a global fellowship working in pursuit of the vision God entrusted to its founder John Stott –

>*to facilitate the growth of the church in maturity and Christ-likeness through raising the standards of biblical preaching and teaching.*

Our vision is to see churches in the majority world equipped for mission and growing to maturity in Christ through the ministry of pastors and leaders who believe, teach and live by the Word of God.

Our mission is to strengthen the ministry of the Word of God through:
- nurturing national movements for biblical preaching
- fostering the creation and distribution of evangelical literature
- enhancing evangelical theological education

especially in countries where churches are under-resourced.

Our ministry

Langham Preaching partners with national leaders to nurture indigenous biblical preaching movements for pastors and lay preachers all around the world. With the support of a team of trainers from many countries, a multi-level programme of seminars provides practical training, and is followed by a programme for training local facilitators. Local preachers' groups and national and regional networks ensure continuity and ongoing development, seeking to build vigorous movements committed to Bible exposition.

Langham Literature provides majority world preachers, scholars and seminary libraries with evangelical books and electronic resources through publishing and distribution, grants and discounts. The programme also fosters the creation of indigenous evangelical books in many languages, through writer's grants, strengthening local evangelical publishing houses, and investment in major regional literature projects, such as one volume Bible commentaries like *The Africa Bible Commentary* and *The South Asia Bible Commentary*.

Langham Scholars provides financial support for evangelical doctoral students from the majority world so that, when they return home, they may train pastors and other Christian leaders with sound, biblical and theological teaching. This programme equips those who equip others. Langham Scholars also works in partnership with majority world seminaries in strengthening evangelical theological education. A growing number of Langham Scholars study in high quality doctoral programmes in the majority world itself. As well as teaching the next generation of pastors, graduated Langham Scholars exercise significant influence through their writing and leadership.

To learn more about Langham Partnership and the work we do visit **langham.org**

Lightning Source UK Ltd.
Milton Keynes UK
UKHW02f0042270918
329577UK00003B/89/P